Promoting Positive Parenting of Teenagers

David Neville
Liz King
Dick Beak

arena

Published by
Arena
Ashgate Publishing Limited
Gower House
Croft Road
Aldershot
Hampshire GU11 3HR
England

Ashgate Publishing Company
Old Post Road
Brookfield
Vermont 05036
USA

British Library Cataloguing in Publication Data
Neville, David, 1949–
   Promoting positive parenting of teenagers
   1. Parenting 2. Parent and teenager 3. Parenting –
   Psychological aspects
   I. Title II. King, Liz III. Beak, Dick
   306.8'74

ISBN 1 85742 425 5

Library of Congress Cataloging-in-Publication Data
Neville, David.
   Promoting positive parenting of teenagers / David Neville, Liz
King, and Dick Beak.
     p. cm.
   Includes bibliographical references.
   ISBN 1–85742–417–4 (pbk.)
   1. Parenting–Study and teaching. 2. Problem children–Behavior
modification–Study and teaching. 3. Parents–Social networks. 4. Family
psychotherapy. 5. Group work in education. I. King, Liz. II. Beak, Dick. III.
Title.
HQ755.7.N48 1998
649'.153'07—dc21

                                     98–19796
                                         CIP

Typeset in Palatino by Bournemouth Colour Press, Parkstone and printed in Great Britain by the University Press, Cambridge.

Dedication

This book is dedicated to Dick Beak, Co-founder of the Centre, who sadly died between its writing and final production. The staff of the Centre for Fun and Families would like to pay tribute to his memory and to record their enormous debt of gratitude for the massive contribution he made to the formation, development and growth of the Centre.

To work with Dick was a rare privilege and immense pleasure. He was our inspiration, our mentor and, equally important, he always made us smile. Through his work he helped us to believe in the ideals that were his. He strove to help parents in distress build better relationships with their children. He wanted to form a voluntary organisation that was a true co-operative, without hierarchy or bureaucracy. He aimed to form supportive working relationships with colleagues, students and other professional staff. Most importantly he believed that work could be fun. It was he who put the 'fun' into Fun and Families!

The staff of the Centre see it as their commitment and aim to ensure that the work he started and that brought him great respect and commendation should continue to flourish and grow.

We shall miss him greatly.

Liz King, Rita Naag and David Neville

Contents

Part III   The seven-week living with teenagers programme

Foreword

Tom Butler, Bishop of Leicester

Being a parent is the hardest job in the world and everybody is willing to criticize you, including your own teenagers. Bringing up teenagers requires amazing patience, tact and the ability to love the unwashed, untidy, uncommunicative and at times the unlovable! However, if you feel you are working with parents who are out of their depth or feel it is all too much, help is at hand. This book, written by the staff of the Centre for Fun and Families, a national voluntary organisation, is about a groupwork programme that has been developed to assist parents who are experiencing behaviour and communication difficulties with their teenagers.

From seven years of experience of running courses for parents, the Centre staff have found that the sorts of behaviours that parents of teenagers are often trying to cope with include violence, swearing, defiance, school refusal, sulking or eating difficulties. However, parents who attend the courses are pleased to find that behaviour difficulties can be reduced by an average of 50% by attending the seven-week course. Most importantly, parents find that the quality of their relationship with their teenagers improves and communication and mutual respect increase as a result.

In addition most parents feel much less anxious because they are able to discover they are not the only ones dealing with these problems. They find that *they* are the real experts on their own teenagers, and that sharing the task of parenting together in a group enables them to discover which of their own solutions work best. Parents meeting together generate tremendous enthusiasm and support which help them achieve very satisfying results. An additional bonus is that those who attend the groups even enjoy them and find them to be fun!

This book has been written as a practice guide for professional staff who work with young people and their families and who want to run groups to assist parents with the hardest but most rewarding job of all – being a positive parent! There has been a great deal of attention amongst politicians and the media in recent years on the subject of parenting. One could be forgiven for thinking that most of the ills of society have their origins in deficiencies in the upbringing of children. Whether this is the case or not this book has a major contribution to make in giving professional staff the means to assist parents who feel they would like a helping hand to make their children's teenage years a positive experience. The book offers a way of working that is tried, tested and carefully evaluated and is relevant to people of all races, cultures and religions. In addition the programme is described in considerable detail and its theoretical and practical bases are rigorously explained.

I welcome this book because it offers a programme that any professional worker can confidently make a start on tomorrow. In doing so staff working with teenagers and their families can make the best possible investment in the future of our society by working to improve the quality of relationships within families.

+ Tom Butler

Acknowledgements

The co-editors would like to thank the following people who have contributed to the development of the 'Living with Teenagers' programme, the work of the Centre and have therefore made this book possible:

- All the professional workers from a variety of agencies with whom we have run groups, for their enthusiasm and support.
- All the social work students who have been on placement at the Centre (40 at the time of writing), and have contributed so much in terms of new ideas and developments.
- All the members of our governing body who have supported us through their encouragement and fund-raising.
- Our Patrons, Sue Townsend, the Right Reverend Tom Butler and Mr and Mrs Vaz for their support.
- Professor Martin Herbert, our Honorary Consultant, whose pioneering and prodigious writing on the subject of behavioural social work and teenagers has been an invaluable guide and encouragement.
- Last, but not least, to our partners who have suffered us while we wrote this book and to our children who have unknowingly given us so many of the ideas that fill its pages.

DN, LK, DB

Introduction
Professor Martin Herbert

When I wrote the introductory chapter for the book *Promoting Positive Parenting* in 1995 I was not surprised to hear that another book was already in the minds of the authors. I have been the Honorary Consultant for the Centre since its formation in 1990 and I have always been impressed by the rate at which the staff of the Centre have been able to convert new ideas into established practice. However, I am delighted and very pleasantly surprised to be writing another introductory chapter so soon because this programme for parents of teenagers represents a further major development in the Centre's group work.

In 1995 I described how the Centre's groupwork programme for parents of children under 12 was based upon well- and empirically-researched theory and practice, validated to improve child behaviours and empower parents. It is collaborative, anti-discriminatory, assists inter-agency co-operation and is effective and economical. If the word teenager were substituted for child my comments then would be equally relevant to the living with teenagers groupwork programme described in this book. What is particularly important about the living with teenagers programme is that it is even more significant for professional staff working in social services and education departments because most of the children entering care or being excluded from school are in the 13- to 16-year age group.

This book, like its successful predecessor, *Promoting Positive Parenting*, offers a step by step, practical guide to the programme and also a thorough introduction to the theoretical ideas that underpin its structure and methodology. The book is neatly divided into four sections. Part I charts the development of the Centre and the living with teenagers groupwork programme. Part II deals with the contribution of theoretical ideas. Of particular relevance in this section is the chapter on specific approaches for dealing with family conflict, including ideas about listening skills, communication skills, negotiation and problem solving and the contribution that written agreements can make to reducing confrontation and tension in families. Part III outlines in detail each of the seven-week sessions of the groupwork programme. Finally Part IV considers issues going beyond the group, including evaluation, parent support groups and the resources available from the Centre to assist and enhance the work. It includes some ideas about future developments and new directions that the staff of the Centre are currently working on.

I would recommend the book to you because the authors have succeeded in conveying a complex but effective model of working in a straightforward and very readable form. Once again they have also made it fun! The living with teenagers groupwork programme has been carefully evaluated and has been shown to be popular and empowering for parents. They feel the service meets the needs of their teenagers and themselves. Consequently, the programme is complementary to the duties local authorities have under the Children Act (1989) to offer support to families and work in partnership with them. The programme is also capable of being made relevant and accessible to parents of any race, culture, religion, gender or disability and the book gives a central place to the theoretical and practical ways this can be achieved, including a case study giving examples of the Centre's work in the area of anti-discriminatory practice. A further benefit of the programme is that it can be run within and by workers from a range of agencies, including social services, education, health, youth work and voluntary agencies. The reader is provided with a range of ideas on the promotion of inter-agency co-working.

The authors of this book are all qualified social workers with wide and long experience in work with children and families. They also have seven years experience of group work with parents and are regularly running living with teenagers groups. Consequently the book is filled with examples of their own day to day work and their experience of offering training and consultancy to professional staff throughout the country. This, plus the authors' obvious enthusiasm for sharing the living with teenagers model with the reader makes the book enormously readable and professionally of great value. I welcome the publication of this book because it offers professional staff a theoretically coherent and validated practical model for work that has the potential to improve the lives of families and their teenagers.

Part I

The background to the Centre
for Fun and Families

1 The development of the Centre

Defining the terms used in this book

This book, *Promoting Positive Parenting of Teenagers*, has been written to give people who work with families and young people a guide to the group programme called 'living with teenagers', developed by the staff of the Centre for Fun and Families. It is important, at the start of this guide, to offer a few definitions of the terms used throughout the book so that the reader can proceed with a common understanding of the language employed. The most important terms you will come across are 'living with teenagers groups', 'social learning theory' and the 'Centre for Fun and Families'. We will start with a brief description of each of these terms.

What is a 'living with teenagers group'?

A living with teenagers group is a seven-week parent training programme designed to help parents whose young people are displaying a range of behaviour difficulties such as aggression, defiance, school refusal, bad language, staying out late, stealing, drug or alcohol abuse. The main objective of the group is to apply social learning theory or behavioural principles to individual family circumstances. It is designed to help parents make sense of what their teenagers are doing and why. It is intended to give practical, down-to-earth suggestions to assist them in changing their teenager's behaviour and to allow them to regain parenthood as a positive or 'fun' experience.

What is social learning theory?

Chapter 4 gives a detailed account of social learning theory. However, the basic assumption of social learning theory is that social behaviour is learned and can be changed by altering the way parents respond to and manage their teenager's behaviour. In simple terms, if parents want to encourage good behaviour they should positively reinforce or reward it, and if they want to reduce unwanted behaviour they should discourage it through a range of methods referred to as 'punishments'. These methods include ignoring, withdrawal of privileges, and so on, which have been shown to be more effective than physical punishments. A range of other means of teaching acceptable social behaviours include modelling, prompting and giving clear instructions. In addition, relationships within families can be improved by attention to skills in listening, communication, negotiation, problem-solving and the use of agreements.

What is the Centre for Fun and Families?

The Centre for Fun and Families is a national voluntary organisation with charitable status (Charity no. 328640), which was established in 1990. The Centre is based in Leicester (25 Shanklin Drive, Knighton, Leicester LE2 3RH, phone 0116 270 7198). The objective of the Centre is to support parents who are experiencing behaviour and communication difficulties with their children and teenagers through the development and promotion of effective groupwork programmes. The Centre offers programmes for parents with young children and parents with teenage children. The programme for parents with younger children is called 'Fun and Families', and the programme for parents with teenage children is called 'Living with Teenagers'.

Within Leicestershire the Centre runs a regular programme of groups for parents in partnership with other agencies such as health visitors, social workers, schools and voluntary organisations. Outside Leicestershire the Centre provides training and consultancy services to both statutory and voluntary agencies throughout the country on the setting up and running of these groupwork programmes. To support these programmes the Centre has produced a range of resources, including 11 booklets, video, a relaxation tape for parents, sets of fun stickers and albums and a parent's guide. The Centre also offers student placements for students on Diploma/MA in Social Work courses to allow them to experience the planning and running of the Centre's groupwork programmes.

The Centre is committed to providing services to people of any race, sex, religion, disability and sexual orientation and has an anti-discriminatory practice policy and action plan.

Information on the details of resources and services available from the Centre are given in Chapter 13 and the Appendices at the end of this book.

The history of the development of the Centre

It can be imagined that the development of a major group programme and the formation of a new voluntary organisation did not occur rapidly or by chance. The ideas came together gradually, piece by piece, between 1987 and 1990 as a result of the convergence of a number of developments.

Development of the fun and families group programme

In 1987 a number of social services staff in south Leicestershire were interested in two themes. First, the application of methods derived from social learning theory were thought to be practical and effective in work with families with child behaviour difficulties. Second, there was an interest both in a community social work approach designed to assist clients in using their own resources and in seeking out resources in the community, such as other agencies, which may have a common interest in helping families.

In terms of the help available to families, health visitors featured prominently. Even before groupwork projects were devised, liaison with health visitors had developed so that meetings and shared workshops were a regular feature. This time spent getting to know, understand and establish a common theoretical base was very significant. Once these simple behavioural ideas were put into practice with parents, a reputation was created in the community that there were practitioners available who could actually help. Equally important, the advice was not overly intrusive and was seen to be effective. The result of this was that more referrals were generated than either the social services staff or health visitors could cope with.

Therefore, in 1987 the first discussions began about setting up groups which could cater for families experiencing difficulty in managing their children's behaviour. Drawing on research and experience, an eight-week programme (later refined to seven weeks) was devised during which parents could learn about and practice techniques with a proven track record in changing child behaviours.

However good any programme is, it would inevitably have a limited impact unless it was presented in an attractive fashion. Therefore, those involved took great pains to offer potential referral sources such as doctors and schools with the programme details and research references so that a high level of credibility was established. Additionally, efforts were made to attract potential clients. An attractive invitation was sent rather than a letter. The first session was to be social with wine and food provided together with the opportunity for participants to comment on the proposed programme and suggest any additions or changes they felt necessary.

The name for the group was also agonised over, and there was a wish to have an attractive title that made the objectives of the group clear. It was recognised that most participants had largely lost the sense of how much fun parents can obtain from bringing up children and were caught in a downward spiral of recrimination, frustration and helplessness. Consequently, the title 'fun and families groups' was born to reflect the group's serious objective of helping families to recapture the lost sense of the fun in bringing up their children.

This aim was pursued with enthusiasm and parents in the early groups taught the organisers a great deal and helped to shape subsequent programmes. Each parent is the only real expert so far as their own child is concerned and it quickly became evident that more time had to be allocated to considering individual circumstances. More time was also allowed for informal discussion (providing it was guided to keep on task) between parents. The encouragement parents drew from each other was also noted as a major feature of the group's effectiveness. Gradually, through the feedback from evaluations of the group, the programme was refined to a seven-week programme in which the minimum necessary theoretical ideas could be presented and the parents' own strengths brought to bear on choosing the best way to achieve positive change for the whole family.

The development of the Centre

Developing an effective group programme that empowers parents in partnership with another agency while working within a busy social services department is a major challenge in itself. Taking this further to develop a completely new voluntary organisation was an even greater challenge and required a unique set of circumstances to prevail.

By 1989 the fun and families group programme had been refined and improved to the point that it had become locally known to parents as an effective and popular group programme to join. In addition, the parent support groups, made up of parents who had already experienced the programme, had felt that similar groups should be set up in other parts of the country. Consequently, they wrote several articles in the local press. Furthermore, Andy Gill, one of the co-founders, wrote an article in the social work press (1989a). The result of all this publicity was that Dick Beak, Andy Gill and the health visitors who had been running the groups began to receive requests for information from agencies all over the country. It rapidly became obvious that the concept of fun and families groups was one that people wanted to know about and a variety of agencies were interested in running similar groups. However, the problem for those involved was how to respond to this while working full time in a statutory setting.

Within the social services department that employed the Centre co-founders there were two ominous forces at work. First, a further reorganisation was pending. Their memory of the previous 1986 reorganisation was that front line services were in some disarray for 12–18 months afterwards and all developmental work was put on hold. Second, the effects of successive Government cutbacks and local policy changes were leading to a situation in which any work with families, other than child protection work, would be impossible to sustain. On the positive side, there was a growing confidence that voluntary organisations would be funded by social services departments, in line with guidance given in the Children Act (1989).

The combination of the above two factors led the co-founders to test the viability of launching a voluntary organisation by producing a questionnaire to all social services departments and members of the Behavioural Social Work Group. They were extremely surprised to find that the response was more than double the expected response for a postal questionnaire, and the replies were all very positive. Taking the idea further, the co-founders held a national conference in Leicester in February 1990. The conference was oversubscribed, attracting over 80 people including almost 20 parents. From these efforts to test demand it was obvious that there was a tremendous interest in the services the Centre hoped to offer.

A further factor of considerable importance was that the three co-founders had worked together since 1987. While all three had different interests and styles of working, they recognised the value of each other's contribution to the concept of the Centre. Consequently, very good working relationships had developed which were going to be essential in guiding a new organisation through the uncharted waters that lay ahead.

Having established, in principle, that the formation of a voluntary organisation was viable, the co-founders needed to solve the last piece of the puzzle; how to fund the organisation. They knew that any new organisation would have high initial set-up costs because of the need to acquire equipment and to publicise and promote the organisation. In addition, the Centre sought to provide training and consultancy, but these could not be relied upon to give a regular, consistent source of income. After considerable searching and discussion it was decided that each co-founder would seek some part-time employment that would give a regular source of income. By March 1990 Dick Beak and David Neville had been accepted to work on the Leicestershire *Guardian ad litem* Panel and Andy Gill was still searching for a part-time post. The decision was taken to launch the Centre on 1 June 1990, with Dick and David starting in June and Andy joining slightly later in November 1990.

The development of the living with teenagers programme

It was evident from the consistently positive evaluations of the fun and families group programmes that parents were highly satisfied with the outcomes of that programme, in terms of the reduction in the number and frequency of child behaviour difficulties. Inevitably parents and professionals began to ask if there was a similar programme for parents of teenagers. Examination showed there was a very clear demand from parents who seemed to find teenage behaviour difficulties even more embarrassing and difficult to deal with than the difficulties presented by younger children.

There was a very obvious need for work with parents of teenagers because most of the young people entering care were in the 14–16-year age range. In addition, a very large proportion of the resources of social services departments were deployed in working with families with teenagers to try to keep such families together. Indeed, many professionals came across increasing numbers of families where, because of rising divorce and remarriage rates, families were coping with both teenagers and toddlers.

Finally, it was apparent that there was a lack of any groupwork programmes dealing directly with influencing teenage behaviour and negotiating for change. Most parenting programmes tended to focus on the under eight age range. At the time of writing the Centre was not aware of any other formally established groupwork programme that was dedicated specifically to parents of teenagers, though there were examples of good practice in working in groups with parents of teenagers dealing with more general issues at a discussion level.

In response to this evidence of need, the Centre staff commenced some development work on a groupwork programme for parents of teenagers during 1991 to 1992. The first step was made when the living with teenagers programme was planned, and in the development meetings the staff became convinced that the main theoretical elements of social learning theory were equally as relevant as they are in the fun and families programme. However, the significant difference that was identified in working with parents of teenagers was that the task of helping parents with the skills of listening, communicating, negotiation and problem solving and being able to use agreements needed to be added to the other existing elements already successfully used to very good effect in the fun and families programme.

During 1993 the Centre's first attempts to run a living with teenagers group began. This was assisted by some finance offered by the Tudor Trust, specifically targeted to develop the programme for work with parents of teenagers. The first group was run in Hinckley in partnership with education welfare officers. The take-up for the first group was small, with only four parents attending. This first group was successful for those who attended but there were two areas that required further work.

It was evident that the take-up by parents of the opportunity to join the group was limited in comparison to the dozen or so parents whose names were put forward. Resistance, it seemed, appeared to come from two sources. First, parents seemed to consider that there was a keenly felt 'stigma' from being viewed as a 'failed' parent. This seemed to be even more pronounced for parents of teenagers since the parents had had responsibility for the care of their young people for between fourteen and sixteen years. They therefore felt that they had to bear some responsibility for their teenagers' behaviour and attitudes. Second, another response that seemed unduly negative was based upon the thought that 'they are nearly sixteen, so there are only a few months before they can leave home, at which point we will be relieved of the difficulties we are experiencing'.

The second area of difficulty was in finding ways of presenting the material in a more interesting way and in finding material that was specific to teenagers. Parents did not seem to be impressed by material that was not directly relevant to their role as parents of teenagers.

However, on the positive side, the parents who had attended had found the groupwork programme useful and this spurred the staff on to continue the development of the programme in the recognition that with further fine tuning the programme had equal potential to the fun and families programme. Consequently, further groups were run in different areas and with different groups of parents. These included:

- 1994   A group run at a community school where the parents had 8–16-year-olds
- 1995   A group run at a women's centre for female single parents of teenagers
- 1996   A group run for Asian fathers of teenagers
- 1997   A group with an open invitation which attracted 13 white parents, of whom six were fathers.

The Centre has now reached the point where the living with teenagers programme has been thoroughly tried and tested and the materials, handouts, video and other materials are now quite distinct from the fun and families programme. Improvements on it will continue to be made, but it has now reached the stage of being a viable groupwork programme with a track record of effectiveness. Its continued development is assured because further funding has been received from the Tudor Trust together with the promise of a three-year grant from the Department of Health to develop further and disseminate information about the programme.

The development and growth of the Centre

In the seven years of the Centre's development between June 1990 and June 1997 there has been very rapid growth and development in the services and resources on offer.

Workshops

The Centre originally commenced its training work with a workshop about 'Setting up and running a fun and families group'. The Centre now has a number of workshop packages on offer. These include the 'Living with Teenagers' programme. Others are on related subjects such as 'Empowerment', 'Promoting Positive Parenting' and 'Promoting Positive Parenting for Foster Carers and Adopters'. Our initial training/consultancy was done in Leicestershire but over the last seven years we have been involved in work across the width and breadth of the United Kingdom.

Student placements

The Centre had no initial plans to offer student placements but the popularity of the placement has led to over 35 students being offered the opportunity to run groups.

Resources

At first there was only one booklet on offer and this was given to group members. Due to the repeated requests for literature to support the training, additional booklets have been written, details of which are given at the end of this book. A relaxation tape for parents has been produced as well as a Parent's Guide to the Fun and Families programme. A particularly pleasing resource are the fun stickers, guidance leaflet and sticker albums which are used in fun and families groups to encourage children's good behaviour. The stickers and album were designed by a parent who had attended a fun and families group run by Andy Gill at the Rugby Family Centre.

Spread of groups

The fun and families groups and living with teenagers groups in Leicestershire were originally only run in Lutterworth and Broughton Astley. However, they have now spread to Hinckley, Wigston, Market Harborough, Melton Mowbray , Loughborough and into the Highfields, St Matthews and Belgrave areas of the city of Leicester.

Multi-cultural expansion

The groups were originally run only for white parents but groups for Asian parents have now been developed. This has led the Centre to produce resources for groupwork in Gujarati and to make a range of partnerships with staff in the Asian community. Further development has taken place to establish groups for African–Caribbean parents and pilot projects have been undertaken. This work has run in parallel to the Centre's development of an anti-discriminatory practice policy and action plan.

The Centre began with three white, male staff. With Andy Gill's departure to work as Project Leader, NSPCC (Portsmouth) in November 1993, the opportunity was taken to remedy the lack of black or female staff. Consequently, Liz King joined the staff in November 1993. In addition, the Centre has two Asian and one white female associate trainers who work on a regular basis. An application for the funding to employ a black trainer has been made to several Trusts.

Fund raising and information distribution

The Centre had an original governing body of three people who applied for charitable status and drew up the Centre's constitution. The governing body now consists of eight female members, three of whom are black, and a male treasurer. There is also a permanent fund raising sub-committee. This sub-committee takes on the role of applying to grant-making trusts and businesses for funds throughout the year and has doubled the grant income of the Centre since it was formed.

Finally, the information about the Centre is much more available and professionally organised. There is now a workshop programme, resources catalogue, student placements booklet and several information booklets for parents.

We hope that this chapter has given you an introduction to the formation, growth and development of the Centre, its fun and families programmes and the social learning theory on which it is based. The rest of this book is intended to give you a guide to all aspects of the theoretical approaches behind our group programme, followed by practical details which include how to plan the group, the groupwork skills required to run it, the content of the weekly session, how to evaluate the work and how to develop continuing support for parents when the group ends. All these matters are considered in the context of anti-discriminatory practice. The final chapter looks at future directions the Centre hopes to take and gives you information on how to seek help if all does not go to plan and how to get in touch with us to tell us when it has all gone very well!

2 Planning a living with teenagers group – practical lessons learned

First thoughts

It is important to bear in mind when thinking about running a living with teenagers group that:

- The most important resources you have are your own skills, experience and local knowledge.
- Each group will be different in some ways so be prepared to be flexible and make changes if problems arise.
- Make sure you give yourself enough time to plan before the group starts and before each session.

We stress the need to draw on your own skill and local knowledge and to feel confident that you can make good use of these. This is because we are aware that some living with teenagers groups have been run in a wide variety of settings, with parents of varying affluence, from different racial and cultural groups and with different proportions of male and female parents. Our experience has been that the group programme seems to be equally effective in most settings but difficulties have most frequently occurred where staff we have trained to run groups have not given sufficient attention to adapting the programme to local circumstances. For example, in parts of west Wales we have been told that it is not possible to run groups during the lambing season; this is because many children do not even go to school at that time because all the family are fully involved in farming activity. Similarly, in Leicester it is important to avoid running groups for Asian parents during Divali, the Hindu equivalent of Christmas and New Year which usually falls some time in October.

Consequently we would urge you to draw on your own skills and knowledge to tackle the issues of racism, sexism and any other forms of discrimination together with your sense of the concerns of your local community, because they are the essential ingredients for running a group on your patch. Examples of the relevance of such knowledge are given throughout this book.

The majority of the material in the rest of this chapter has been derived from discussions and contributions made at conferences and workshops held in parts of the country as far apart as Carmarthenshire, Guernsey and Essex. The material can serve as a checklist of matters that need to be attended to in the successful planning of a group. The important task for you is to undertake the planning of these matters while bearing in mind the nature and context of the environment in which you are working.

A planning checklist

It is useful to have an initial checklist of all the items that require thought before the group starts. From our experience most workers who are running a living with teenagers group for the first time need about two to three months to make sure all these matters have been dealt with. However, workers running subsequent groups can often complete the planning process in four to six weeks. In the rest of this chapter we will list the issues that usually need to be considered and give some thought on how plans can be made to resolve them.

Size of group

Experience suggests that a group size of about eight to ten people is ideal. This is most likely to consist of perhaps one or two couples and four to six individuals. If the group is bigger, individuals, particularly the least able or vocal, tend to get lost and their concerns are not fully addressed. If the group is smaller it tends to lack the range of experience and tends to become more prone to domination by one or two individuals. Another feature with small groups of, for example, less than six, is that if one or two people don't attend, the group is in danger of folding up. We have recently had some experience of running groups for 12 to 15 people. This can work but it has required the use of three co-leaders. In addition, it has been noticeable that, while the overall evaluation for the group has been just as good as smaller groups, there is a tendency for people who are less able, due to lack of social or literacy skills or intellectual difficulties, to do less well in larger groups.

Consequently, if you know in advance that the people you are going to work with might be more limited, it is preferable to aim for a smaller group size.

Composition of the group

Before thinking about the composition of the group a fundamental question arises that the reader may wish to ponder. In our work with parents of younger children in fun and families groups we focus our work upon parents. Consequently, the children do not attend the groups. However, there is a strong argument that as the child becomes a teenager and is able to take on more responsibility they should be able to attend the groups. However, there are practical reasons why it has not been possible, as yet, to arrange this in groups that we have run.

At the start of groups parent and teenager relationships are often strained to breaking point so that it is not often possible to contemplate how they could be effectively worked with alongside other parents and teenagers. Parents of teenagers often express the view that the two-hour weekly sessions are valuable to them as oases of tranquillity and that they would find it difficult to see how the sessions would work with their teenagers present. Furthermore, having teenagers present would reduce the number of parents able to attend the group since it is very difficult to work with more than 12 individuals at once.

We are, nonetheless, of the view that the more involved the teenager is in the process of improving family relationships, the more effective the group programme will be, and we have tried several ideas to involve teenagers. Consequently, parents are encouraged to share the weekly material they acquire from the group with their teenagers. This has often proved very valuable in terms of improving communication.

In the later sessions (Sessions 3, 4 and 5) many of the exercises, such as those involving the use of written agreements, do rely upon parents and teenagers sitting down together and sharing with each other ideas about the things they would both like to improve in terms of the quality of family relationships.

In discussions we have had with professional staff and parents the idea of running a parallel group for the teenagers at the same time as the living with teenagers group has been proposed. We have not pursued this idea yet because it would be very time-consuming and a lot of thought would be needed about what would actually be included in the teenagers' group sessions. In addition, we would need to think long and hard about how we would attract the teenagers to such a group! However, it is important to consider the feasibility of involving teenagers themselves.

There are several other matters that need to be considered in terms of group composition. These include race, gender, age of the teenagers and the nature of the behaviours about which the parent is concerned. The issues of race and gender will be dealt with later in this chapter.

In terms of the age of the teenagers, experience has suggested that running groups for parents with teenagers of widely varying ages is difficult and probably less effective. However, the age at which a child is considered to be a 'teenager' can be very variable. Certainly our experience has been that some parents with very mature 10-year-olds can work effectively in groups with parents of immature 13-year-olds. We have found that parents of teenagers need to focus on similar social learning theory principles to those used in fun and families groups, but skills in listening, communication, problem solving and negotiation become much more important.

At some point a decision may have to be made between suggesting to a parent that they join a fun and families group or a living with teenagers group. A general rule of thumb would be to talk to the parent about a child or young person's maturity and the sort of behaviours that the child or young person is displaying. Having that information would then help the reader to direct the parent to the most appropriate group. A further factor to consider is whether there are likely to be other parents with children under the age of 13 in the group. If there are then it is probably useful for the parent to join a living with teenagers group since they would not feel too isolated.

There does seem to be an advantage, if possible, in running a group with parents who are experiencing a range of different degrees of severity of behaviour difficulty. For example, running a group solely for parents who have children in care or at risk of entering local authority accommodation may present problems. Such a group may have greater initial negativity and helplessness which may inhibit progress. There may also be greater worries from parents about stigma, especially if their attendance has any degree of coercion or compulsion about it. Our experience has been that a mix of parents, some of whom are experiencing the risk of family breakdown and some who are experiencing less severe difficulties, is most productive. Such a mix can best be achieved by encouraging referrals from a range of sources, including self-referrals. The latter are usefully encouraged through local press articles. An example of an article that was placed in local newspapers is included for your information in the Appendices. Your local knowledge of other agencies and their readiness to refer is important here. Generally, social services departments and schools have access to a wide range of potential referrals.

Where to run a group

Generally speaking, groups seem to be most successful when they are run in premises that are neutral or non-threatening. Community centres, or other types of facility that do not stigmatise participants are useful. Social services offices, schools or other premises associated with formal agencies can be extremely off-putting to parents. However, local knowledge is again vital when planning for your venue because some premises can be a great deal more welcoming than others. For example, we recently ran a group in a school because it had good facilities, including a kitchen and a very informal adult lounge. The most important factor seemed to be that the entrance to the lounge was next to swimming baths and it was therefore easy for parents to enter without being stigmatised by attending a particular class. Also, if you are attempting to attract people from different racial and cultural backgrounds you need to be sensitive about the significance for the parents of the location you choose. Some locations also have other advantages. Family centres can often provide childcare facilities for parents which can be a great asset. However, the need for a crèche seems to be much less important for parents attending living with teenagers groups. In rural areas, where transport can be a major obstacle, a location offering access to public transport can be useful.

When to run a group

There are varying advantages according to whether you plan to run a group in the evening or during the working day. The advantages of evening groups seem to be:

- It is possible for parents who work to come to such groups although, in itself, it does not guarantee their attendance.
- It also seems possible to develop the informal, social element of the group more effectively.
- Other work pressures are less likely to interfere with the running of the group, assuming you have the energy left at the end of a draining day to run a group!

The advantages of daytime groups appear to be:

- You can do it in work time!
- Childcare (if necessary) and transport facilities are easier to arrange.
- Other professional staff may be happier to work with you during the day.

From the experience of trying a range of different times, the most consistently successful seems to be 6.30pm, or 7pm to 8.30pm or 9pm. The afternoon presents problems because of the need for parents to pick up younger children from school.

Who to run a group with

There are a wide variety of professional staff who become involved in work with teenagers and their families. We are aware of a range of groups being run by social workers and resource centre staff, workers from voluntary agencies, educational psychologists and social workers and their colleagues from child guidance units or education welfare officers. Such partnerships in running groups make great sense because, apart from the obvious advantage of sharing professional skills, time, experience and mutual support, it is possible to share:

- Premises and equipment, for example video, flip charts or photocopying
- Transport
- Referral sources
- Costs of planning and running a group
- Publicity
- Female or male workers or workers from a variety of races
- Childcare facilities, if necessary.

Another useful spin-off is that inter-agency relationships often improve very dramatically when a new, positive innovation in working practice is shared. This spin-off should not be underestimated. The improvement in working relationships and the consequent raising of morale can dramatically reduce the workload and cut down on frustrating and time-consuming wrangles that are often the bane of our lives in the caring professions.

The list below is a good prompt to help you to use your local information to think of all the professional staff who might work with children and families who are experiencing behaviour difficulties:

- Youth workers
- Child guidance
- School nurses
- Resource centre staff
- Social workers
- Family service unit
- Education welfare
- NSPCC
- Special needs teachers.

Publicity – how to attract families

From the experience of running groups for over seven years it is apparent that word of mouth recommendations of the effectiveness of the groupwork are the best publicity medium. However, that is not a lot of help to you when you are planning your first group!

There are a number of options you can select. First, co-working with other agencies is very helpful since other professionals will be aware of families who might benefit from referral to a living with teenagers group. Second, it is helpful to use local publications, newspapers or community newspapers. Again, your local knowledge and contacts are vital here because you need to make sure that the local press will actually print what you want so that a positive image of the group can be fostered. Finally, the use of leaflets and posters also works but it needs to be stressed that these must be located where the parents you want to attract will see them. Doctors' surgeries, newsagents, libraries, community centres and schools can be good locations. Publicising the group through other professionals can also be a good idea.

Remember, in your publicity effort, that social services departments and other statutory agencies are a source of fear for many parents and their anxieties have been raised by the media. It is therefore essential to stress a positive and helpful image in your publicity material. This is not an approach that professionals are given much opportunity to practice but the Centre has a range of examples of newspaper articles about living with teenagers that are available, upon request.

The place of evaluation in your group programme

There are many good reasons for planning to evaluate your groupwork with parents:

- Your managers will want to know how effective your groupwork is.
- It helps parents to see how much they have achieved.
- It helps you to assess whether some approaches work better than others.
- Finally, it is always good practice to evaluate what you do, and it conveys a sense of professionalism and care about quality to parents.

The evaluation can simply consist of establishing a 'baseline'. This is achieved by obtaining the parent's rating of their teenager's behaviour prior to the start of the group and comparing this with the parent's assessment when the group has finished. This can be done by using a teenager's behaviour rating scale, of which there are many available. The Centre has produced its own and an example of it is in the Appendices. (Further copies of the questionnaire can be obtained from the Centre.) There is also one in Herbert (1988, p. 17).

Contact with families before the group

Our experience would suggest that home visits prior to the group are *essential*, preferably by one or more of the group leaders. We would stress that neglecting home visits has been the most frequent cause of group failure, because hardly anyone turned up to the first session. The home visit serves a number of purposes:

- It ensures that the parents have met at least one group leader prior to the group's first session.
- It raises the parent's enthusiasm for the group and ensures that the parents have sorted out the potential problems of child care or transport which could prevent them arriving at the group.
- It enables the group leaders to check out that the group programme is the best way to offer help to that particular family.
- Where there are problems with literacy or disability plans can be made in advance to deal with these factors tactfully and effectively within the group sessions.
- Any matters in relation to the family's race or culture, or a family member's gender or disability can be noted in order to make the group as relevant as possible to each individual parent.
- It gives the opportunity to commence the evaluation by asking the parents to complete the teenage behaviour Rating Scale (see section on evaluation above).
- Home visits give the opportunity to meet parents and to try to persuade both parents (when there are two of them) to attend.

In view of the fact that 30–40% of the parents who attended the most recent living with teenagers group were male the home visit is clearly an effective strategy in persuading both parents to attend.

Transport, child care and refreshments

These very practical issues are clearly matters that rely on local knowledge and circumstances, but they can make all the difference to the effective running of the group so do not neglect them. We have found, however, that the provision of crèche facilities has not seemed to be very significant in persuading parents to keep coming along to a living with teenagers group.

Refreshments are an important part of creating a warm, welcoming atmosphere and help to establish the informal side of the group's task. This is very important when you bear in mind the considerable anxiety most parents feel when first attending a group. It is also important to make sure that you think about the right type of refreshments, especially if you are aware from your home visits that black or Asian families are attending the group.

One group run by Resource Centre staff recently had very poor attendance because transport was not offered. When feedback from those not attending was received it was clear that the prospect of getting to the group in a rural area on public transport, involving several changes of buses, was just too much to cope with. Although providing transport for each session might seem a large drain on resources our experience has been that if you can get parents to the first session they will often team up with other parents to share lifts for subsequent sessions.

Obtaining commitment and funding from managers

While this may not be a planning problem for all workers it is an important consideration that sometimes needs to be tackled. Where this is the case the lack of funding or commitment from managers can undermine all the other good work you have already done.

In order to assist in the process of convincing your managers that running living with teenagers groups is a good idea we have developed a list of arguments based on the word 'changes':

> Cost effective – helps ten families at once, uses parents as resources and can be run with others
> Here and now – focus is on each parent's agenda and change can be achieved within the seven weeks
> Anxiety and stress reducing – parents regain control, and family and individual stress is reduced
> Networks – informal support of parents develops and networking with other agencies grows
> Growth of confidence – group programme empowers parents to tackle other issues in their lives
> Evidence of effectiveness – evaluations demonstrate consistent reductions in poor teenage behaviour
> Sharing of skills and resources with other agencies – creates good inter-agency relationships.

You may find it useful to add other items according to local circumstances while retaining the central arguments.

Funding is very much a matter of local budgeting practice but a few general points can be made:

- The major cost involved in running a living with teenagers group is staff time which is normally already paid for, so the additional costs tend to be for publicity, refreshments, handouts, booklets for parents and photocopying. Again, many of these are already available in larger statutory or voluntary agencies. A recent estimate done for an agency was that running a living with teenagers group would take roughly 32 hours over a four-month period to plan, do home visits and run the group. This would work out at between two and three hours per week.

- Two agencies working together can give you access to double the sources of funding.
- Where there are outstanding costs, other than staff time, the sources to meet these can include the following:

1) Preventive aid money under Section 17 of the Children Act 1989, used on the grounds that teenagers are being prevented from coming into care. If parents with teenagers who are at risk of being accommodated attend the group, there is a very strong argument for the use of this type of funding.

2) Voluntary agencies can sometimes obtain seed money or small grants to start up new projects.

3) Many agencies have book budgets, play equipment or other budgets which can provide some of the resources needed.

4) Finally, some agencies have reprographic departments which can produce leaflets or posters at low or no cost, providing your managers sanction it. However, they can take three to four weeks to produce so plan ahead!

- Charities or grant-making trusts are not an ideal source of funding but if you do have a good local contact they can often produce the small sums necessary for non-staff resources.

Race, gender, disability and sexual orientation

The Centre has a commitment to anti-discriminatory practice and great effort has been made to promote good practice in groupwork in such a way as to demonstrate that commitment. Before looking in detail at ways in which these issues can begin to be addressed in the planning of a group programme, it is worth looking at some of the basic assumptions of the living with teenagers group programme that can assist you in developing anti-discriminatory practice.

The most important point to stress is that in living with teenagers groups the parents are the key people in setting the agenda for change. There is no question, therefore, of telling parents which behaviours to alter or how to alter the behaviour. The purpose of the groups is to help parents define for themselves exactly *what* behaviour they want to change, to develop their own understanding of *why* that particular behaviour occurs and to select, from a range of options, *how* to change their teenager's behaviour. In theory such an approach is not 'value laden' and should be accepting of the social, cultural and religious values of any parent.

In planning a group it is important to promote anti-discriminatory attitudes. In discussions in staff and student meetings it has been concluded that the most effective way to do this is to include in the first session a discussion of the aims of the group; this would permit the opportunity to outline briefly the Centre's commitment to avoiding any racist, sexist or discriminatory language of any sort. In addition it is important to ensure that your presentation and material offers positive images of black people, women, people with disabilities, gay people and other minority groups that suffer discrimination.

Race issues

The view of the Centre is that it is vital that groupwork approaches, as a means of offering help to parents experiencing behaviour difficulties with their teenagers, should be available to people of all races. We are committed to offering this service and are running groups in the Leicester area for Asian and African-Caribbean families, in cooperation with other statutory agencies such as health visitors, social workers and schools. In the rest of this section when we use the word 'black' we are using it as a short way of referring to any person who is not white.

The following ideas are derived from our experience, discussions that have taken place on workshops and our own anti-racist training:

Ideal strategies

It is preferable to start your thinking from the point of looking at the ideal way to run a group that will attract people from all races, and then to consider other options that might be possible if ideal conditions do not exist.

Ideally, the best way to run a group that will include people from different races is to ensure that the group leaders are representative of the races of the catchment area of the group. This will most probably involve seeking out group leaders from the Asian or African-Caribbean communities. This approach is most preferable because:

- The group leaders will have a good knowledge of the needs, wishes and aspirations of those communities. Such knowledge will greatly assist the process of communication and help in raising the enthusiasm for the group in those communities.

- Co-working with group leaders from different races will help to attain a presentation and choice of material that does not fall foul of the personal bias and prejudice that we all carry. The planning process will be assisted on such matters as where and when to run a group and how to publicise the group because of the workers' knowledge of their own community.
- The co-working of group leaders from different races makes a clear and obvious statement about your agency's intentions to run anti-discriminatory services for a multi-racial community.
- Most importantly, our experience is that working with black staff is the most effective way of ensuring that you are successful in attracting and retaining black families to the group programme. This is because Asian and African-Caribbean parents find the group programme most relevant to their needs if the group leaders are representative of their community.

Other options

Due to the impact of institutional racism it may not be possible to locate black workers in your agency to co-work with you in running a group. It is also not always possible for black workers to offer the required time since they may have other priorities that are equally demanding of their attention. We recognise that excessive demands upon black colleagues may lead to us abusing them. Finally, some black workers may feel that they have not the necessary skills, experience or time to co-run a group.

It is quite possible, however, to locate black workers in other agencies who may be able to assist. There may also be local voluntary agencies who can help. Once again your local contacts and knowledge are invaluable in this search.

If, after an exhaustive search to find black workers, or to obtain their help, you are not successful, there are two other possible options:

- Seek the assistance of respected figures in the black community. Although they may not have the necessary skills or wish to act as group leaders, they will be able to make invaluable contributions to the group programme and give the work of the group greater credibility.
- Seek the help of black parents with whom you may have worked in another capacity, such as a volunteer or as a parent in a living with teenagers group. It would be particularly useful if they had some understanding of the nature of the groupwork programme.

Overall, it has to be said that these other options are second-best. Our experience is that they are much less likely to work. Also, we feel that our long-run objective should be to develop expertise in running living with teenagers groups among black workers, and this is going to be most rapidly achieved by working with black staff from the outset.

Gender issues

There seem to be two main areas concerning gender that need to be given attention when planning a group:

- The need to persuade both parents to come to the group, thereby acknowledging that the care of their children is a joint responsibility.
- The need to address prevailing sexist attitudes in society through the inclusion of relevant material in the groupwork programme designed to promote non-sexist approaches to child care.

Parental attendance

Professional staff, when running groups, have had varying success in achieving the attendance of both parents or carers. Our groups have rarely managed to attain more than 25%–30% male attendance, although a recent living with teenagers group achieved a 45% male attendance. Consequently, it is not possible to offer any tried or tested formula for success. However, daytime groups seem to have the lowest rate of success in attracting male partners. Despite this there are many daytime groups that do attract men who either work shifts or are unemployed.

We are coming to the view that greater success will be achieved if a specific effort is made at the home visit stage to include both carers in the discussions. In particular, this is likely to be effective because it will help raise the enthusiasm of both partners and also help them to understand the importance of their attendance at the group. It will also help both parents to set to work on solving the problems of childcare arrangements, since one of the most common excuses for non-attendance given by male partners is that they have to stay at home to care for their children! Another important factor seems to be the co-working of a female and male group leader so that men do not feel either 'isolated' or that they are attending a 'women's group'. There is also the need to address prevailing sexist attitudes in society through the inclusion of relevant material in the groupwork programme designed to promote non-sexist approaches to child care.

It is worth stating that there may be some circumstances in which workers may wish to plan deliberately for an all-female (or all-male) group. For example, the Centre recently ran a living with teenagers group for Asian fathers of teenagers. If this is the case it would be worth spending time looking at the content of the programme and making necessary changes, since the programme has been structured on the assumption of a mix of male and female parents.

Promoting non-sexist attitudes

Group discussions with parents over seven sessions will almost inevitably raise some issues about prevailing sexist attitudes in society. However, if you are committed to non-sexist practice you will want to introduce some material at strategic points in the programme in order to make sure the issue is addressed.

From discussions we have had on this subject there seem to be preferred places in the programme to introduce ideas about the different ways that females and males are treated in families. For example, in the second session of the group, we begin by looking at the concept of what is 'normal' behaviour for teenagers. This seems a good point to ask the group to look at whether they find some behaviour more acceptable for girls than for boys and to look at how these attitudes might have arisen. In addition, in session five, where parent's thoughts and feelings and dealing with stress are considered, the need to share responsibilities and support each other can be usefully raised.

It is also important to check and reflect on all the material you might use to make sure that it does not inadvertently reinforce sexist stereotypes. It is equally important to be prepared to challenge any sexist or other offensive statements made in the group in such a way that makes clear your commitment to anti-discriminatory practice.

Disability

Over the last year the Centre has been very active in developing a groupwork programme for parents of children with disabilities. This was greatly assisted by having a Diploma in Social Work student on placement with us who had a child with attention deficit disorder. The student helped to focus our minds on the issues raised for parents in caring for children with disabilities and also stimulated us to gather as much written material as possible on the subject. In turn this led us to produce a booklet entitled 'Working with parents with children with disabilities'.

Sexual orientation

In terms of lessons learned, the Centre has no direct experience of running groups for gay parents of teenagers, although it is part of our anti-discriminatory practice policy action plan to do so as soon as possible.

In the light of our lack of practical experience in running groups for gay parents of teenagers, it was not felt helpful to attempt to offer specific practical guidelines. However, Chapter 3 offers a general theoretical framework that should assist in planning such a group.

Clearly, the area of groupwork dealing with anti-discriminatory practice requires considerable skill and sensitivity and requires careful planning to achieve good practice. We have found that some staff and students can allow this area of work to become so anxiety provoking and contentious that the eventual outcome is that nothing is achieved or attempted. This seems to be the worst outcome of all! But it is important not to feel discouraged, because you are more likely to run into problems due to inadequate planning than you are through making a few mistakes.

Part II

Theoretical background to practice

3 Empowerment and anti-discriminatory practice

During the development of the living with teenagers programme and the development of the Centre, the two themes of empowerment and anti-discriminatory practice have been central to our thinking and action. We will look at each of these concepts in turn and at the theoretical background and practical implications of these for our living with teenagers groupwork programme. The practical application of these theoretical concepts to the living with teenagers programme is dealt with in detail in Chapters 8–13.

Empowerment

We will first offer a definition of empowerment, then consider the expected outcomes of empowering parents, look at the empowering aspects of the living with teenagers programme and finally look at the evidence that these outcomes occur for parents attending living with teenagers groups.

Definition of empowerment

The concepts of user involvement, participation, partnership and empowerment are all, to some degree, interchangeable and all present considerable difficulty in being precisely and acceptably defined. For the purposes of the work of the Centre we have used the definition offered by Beresford and Croft (1990): 'making it possible for people who are disempowered to exercise power and to have more control over their lives. This means having a greater voice in institutions, agencies and situations that effect them' (p. 47).

An alternative and more comprehensive definition is offered by a combination of definitions offered by Adams (1990) and Solomon (1976): 'Empowerment is a process whereby staff engage in a set of activities with individuals, groups and communities. The aim of these activities is to reduce powerlessness, to allow individuals, groups or communities to perceive themselves as forces capable of exerting influence, thereby being able to achieve their own goals and work towards maximising the quality of their own lives.'

Expected outcomes of empowering parents

From a literature search on the anticipated outcomes of empowering parents, the following are thought to result from increasing the influence parents have on a service:

- Parents attain increased dignity and self-respect.
- Decision-making about individual services are based on the best, most accurate, information.
- Services are more appropriate to parents' needs.
- Parents' problem-solving skills are improved.
- Greater diversity and choice of services develop to meet parents' needs more appropriately.
- Forward planning of services is based upon the best information and therefore more accurately reflects clients' needs.

Empowering aspects of the living with teenagers group programme

Various aspects of the living with teenagers groupwork programme are instrumental in empowering parents who attend. First, parents are able to choose for themselves the behaviours they want to change and are also able to select for themselves the methods, from a range of alternatives, that they wish to use to achieve behaviour change. Second, parents can offer and receive support from other parents. This is actively encouraged by group leaders, both in the programme and also in the design of the activities and exercises.

The approach of social learning theory does not apportion blame for behaviours but offers ways of defining and understanding behaviour which can assist parents to develop practical strategies for change. Therefore it does not make parents feel they have 'failed' or that they are 'problem parents'. This removes the stigma or moral sting of failure and thus improves parents' self-esteem. The language and methods used in the programme are down-to-earth, free of jargon, require the minimum of literacy skills and are designed to be non-threatening and supportive and even fun!

There is an emphasis on not keeping any records of the group, except basic factual details such as name, address and phone number. The only other material that is kept relates to the evaluation of the group, usually kept anonymously in the form of Parent 1, Parent 2, etc. This makes parents feel that they are in control of the information they offer in the group.

It is also important that the parents are aware that the programme has been consistently evaluated to have a high success rate which builds parental confidence that positive change can be achieved. Additionally, the step by step practical approach plus the emphasis in the fifth session on offering positive challenges to negative thoughts and feelings, greatly enhances parents' feelings of confidence and self-esteem.

Finally, there is a very strong emphasis in the first session on developing an encouraging, approachable and friendly group atmosphere. The aims of the group are clearly set out and parents are offered the opportunity to participate in voicing their expectations of what should happen in the group. For example, a group of Asian fathers of teenagers requested that we offer an additional session on drugs. This was accommodated within the programme after a hasty trip to the Health Education Library!

Do living with teenagers groups empower parents and are the expected outcomes achieved?

An important question that has been raised throughout the development of the living with teenagers programme has been whether the programme succeeds in achieving the outcomes expected from the process of empowering parents and their teenagers. The Centre was greatly assisted in trying to answer this question by Andy Gill (the Centre co-founder) in his Ph.D research project which was designed to look at the key elements of the fun and families group programme that made it effective for parents.

However, one of the different questions that arises in thinking about the living with teenagers programme is whether the outcomes for parents are equally applicable to their teenagers. It would be hoped that the improvements in relationships within the family would be passed on to the teenagers. A research project by Trevor Collumbell, a Diploma in Social Work student who had a placement at the Centre, offers some interesting evidence on this subject. He interviewed six Asian fathers who had taken part in a living with teenagers group in February/March 1996, six months after the group had finished. The responses from the parents were : 'Parents understood their teenagers and their point of view better. Communication, listening and mutual respect were all improved. Parents and their teenagers talked more and parents became more aware of teenagers' rights and the pressures they were under by listening to them, talking and taking time to understand their needs, and the demands upon them from society at large.'

In answering the question we have posed it is useful to look in turn at each of the expected outcomes of empowering parents and to look at the evidence for the assertion that living with teenagers groups do succeed in empowering parents.

Increased dignity and self-respect

It is clear from the comments parents have made on the research questionnaires that they feel much better about themselves and what they have achieved by the end of a living with teenagers group. Comments on this subject have included:

- 'The course has taught me to be a good listener and to pay more attention to what the children may be saying. It also helps me to be more tolerant and patient and it has helped in improving the "behaviour" – both mine and my teenager's.'
- 'Before attending the course I felt totally helpless and alone. Being able to share difficulties and get practical advice that works has helped me to be less confused and more confident about the future.'
- 'I can see now that my difficulties are not as unusual or bad as I thought. This helps.'

Decision-making about individual services are based upon the best, most accurate information

Decisions about which behaviour to change and which method to use are made by parents themselves. It is therefore inevitable that this outcome will be achieved, since the parent is given the role of 'expert' on their own teenager and family. This is particularly empowering to parents from different races or cultures who may otherwise feel that their own values and views are being overlooked.

Services are more appropriate to parents' needs

Andy Gill found, from his research, that there was a similarity and predictability in parental needs and experiences. Most parents, prior to joining a group, complained of isolation, confusion, helplessness and frustration in response to their children's behaviour. Parents expressed a wish to have an investment in prevention rather than crisis intervention. The living with teenagers group programme offers a preventative approach which has the potential to meet the needs of both statutory agencies, parents, and teenagers. Studies on the services offered to teenagers and their families showed that social workers saw their intervention as an opportunity to work on developmental needs, families wanted their teenagers controlled and young people looked for practical solutions (Department of Health, 1996). The living with teenagers programme has the potential to meet all of these aspirations.

In addition, through the process of evaluation (see Part IV) parents are able to offer feedback to improve the services on offer. For example, the Centre is developing a 'Parents' Manual' so that parents have a method of keeping all the handouts and booklets in a sturdy folder. This is in response to parents finding difficulty in keeping them all in one place or trying to keep prying hands or dogs' teeth off them!

Problem-solving skills are improved

It is evident from the evaluation results of successive living with teenagers groups that the average 50% reduction in teenage behaviour difficulties achieved by parents is a reflection of the increased problem-solving skills of parents who have attended a group. Some examples of parents comments on this include: 'Made me realise that other parents face similar problems and talking with other fathers about their experiences broadened my views and understanding. Helped me to communicate better with my teenagers,' also 'When I started the course I was hard-headed but in the end the course has made me see things in a different light. Very good course,' and 'The course has been quite helpful. Some of the things I learnt during the course were put into practice and it worked.'

A very common and understandable question about the evaluation results is whether the improved problem-solving skills are sustained over time. Andy Gill's research project (1997) involved interviewing and testing how well parents were retaining the progress they had made after three months, six months and every six months, until three years had elapsed. His research showed that parents did continue to hold on to the progress made, although there was inevitably some degree of deterioration. There is a fuller discussion of the reasons for this and why certain parents seem to hold on to the progress better than others in Part IV.

One of the common criticisms of groupwork is that it does not change the status quo. However, there have been some interesting examples of how parents, having regained their sense of control and self-esteem, begin to tackle matters beyond child behaviour. One set of three parents who attended a fun and families group in Bradford all lived in temporary council accommodation. They came to recognise, during the process of the group, that they had gone as far as they could to improve their children's behaviour. However, their accommodation was hampering them because of its poor condition, including rotting and unsafe windows, leaking plumbing and a number of other faults. Consequently, the three parents wrote a joint letter asking for an appointment to see the Chair of the Housing Committee to request improvements to their housing conditions. This example demonstrates that the fun and families group programme can help parents to develop strategies for change beyond simply changing their children's behaviour, and therefore has the potential to change the status quo.

Greater diversity and choice of services develops to meet parents' needs more appropriately

The fun and families groupwork programme developed from one programme to offer services to Asian parents, to a groupwork programme for parents of teenagers and a programme for parents with children with special needs. In addition the Centre has positively responded to parents' needs to have a female worker (Liz King) at the Centre.

Forward planning of services is based upon the best information and therefore more accurately reflects parents' needs

Information about parents' views are obtained from the feedback on the evaluation forms, through discussions at parent support groups and from parents who serve on the Centre's governing body. From these sources changes and improvements have been made to the programme over the period the programme has been running.

Hopefully, this section on empowerment has given you a clear theoretical view of empowerment and offered guidelines for the types of approach to running living with teenagers groups that are likely to empower parents.

Anti-discriminatory practice

During the development of the living with teenagers group programme and the development of the Centre, the theme of anti-discriminatory practice has been central to our thinking and action. In the process of creating our policies and practices we have come to conclude that 'Anti-discriminatory practice is therefore not an optional extra, but an essential part of good practice' (Anderson, Osada and Thompson, 1994, p. 17). In addition 'There is no comfortable middle ground; intervention either adds to oppression (or at least condones it) or goes some small way towards easing or breaking such oppression. In this respect the political slogan, "If you're not part of the solution, you must be part of the problem", is particularly accurate' (Anderson, Osada and Thompson, 1994, p. 16).

This section looks at these concepts and examines their theoretical background and practical implications for our living with teenagers groupwork programme. It concludes with a case study of the Centre's attempts to run groups for Asian parents in Leicester and includes a critical commentary on the successes achieved and failures experienced.

Definition

Anti-discriminatory practice has been defined as 'an approach to social work practice which seeks to reduce, undermine or eliminate discrimination and oppression, specifically in terms of challenging sexism, racism, ageism and disablism and other forms of discrimination encountered in social work' (Thompson, 1993, p. 31).

This section considers how such practice can be put into action in running a living with teenagers group. This can best be approached from a theoretical perspective by looking at the positive actions that any organisation, team or individual can take to achieve its task or activity. These can include activities which include:

- Raising awareness
- Working in partnership with others and acting collectively
- Having a clear theoretical base to work from
- Keeping anti-discriminatory practice as a central issue, not an optional or additional focus
- Being prepared to monitor, evaluate and be critical of your practice, and to attempt to learn and change in response to feedback.

With these theoretical guidelines for action it is helpful to look at how each of these positive activities can be achieved in the process of planning and running a living with teenagers group programme. It is worth repeating that these can only be general guidelines which need to take account of local conditions and circumstances.

Raising awareness

Within the process of planning a living with teenagers group the following can raise awareness of issues of discrimination:

- Publicity material can be a medium for offering positive images of people who suffer discrimination. This can be in terms of language, pictures or logos used.
- Home visits give an opportunity to refer to your organisation's anti-discriminatory practice policy.

- The locations you might choose to run your groups in can be used to raise awareness; for example, if you can select a venue that has facilities for people with disabilities.
- By planning to actively involve male partners in your group you are making a statement about men's equal responsibility for childcare. Alternatively, running an all-female group and focusing on awareness raising and empowerment of women can change people's views.
- Planning to run groups for people of different races in your area is a good way to raise your agency's and your own awareness of their needs.
- In co-working with other agencies, anti-discriminatory practice can be promoted.

During the running of a living with teenagers group the following suggestions can be made to raise awareness:

- During the first session parents can be made aware of and can contribute to establishing the goals for the group which can include a commitment to anti-discriminatory practice. This can be reinforced in subsequent discussions in later sessions.
- Ensure that all handouts, videos, booklets, games and exercises offer positive images of people who suffer discrimination and contain no implicitly discriminatory material.
- Ensure that translations of written material are available. In addition co-work with colleagues who can interpret in languages spoken by parents who live in your area or arrange for interpreters/signers.

Working in partnership with others and acting collectively

The successful running of living with teenagers groups almost inevitably involves other workers and agencies. This is most likely to occur in either seeking premises, seeking a co-worker, providing childcare facilities or finding ways of either publicising or seeking referrals for your group. Through your contact with such workers and agencies it is possible to support the efforts of others who want to practice in an anti-discriminatory way. Examples of this might include supporting a worker who has been trying to persuade their management committee to provide access to their premises for people with disabilities, or writing a letter of support for the continuation of a project you have worked with that provides services for black families.

Having a clear theoretical base to work from

It is very important to be able to explain clearly why you might choose a particular course of action when running a living with teenagers group. It is essential that practice be based upon a clear and explicit theory base 'in order to be able to swim against the dominant tide of discriminatory assumptions' (Thompson; 1993, p. 153). Such a good theoretical base will give you the insight, for example, when proofreading a handout from a colleague or co-worker stating 'because of "manpower" shortages it is a "black day" for the "disabled" and the "elderly"', that this can be rewritten 'because of staff shortages it is a depressing day for people with disabilities and older people'.

Keeping anti-discriminatory practice as a central focus

When running a living with teenagers group several steps can be taken to maintain anti-discriminatory practice as a central rather than as an additional focus:

- Drawing parents' attention to your anti-discriminatory practice policy in the first session, and then making sure that all your materials retain the theme of positive images of people who are discriminated against, will give it a central focus.
- Co-working with people from disadvantaged groups is more likely to assist you in presenting material in an anti-discriminatory way.
- Making sure your agency has an anti-discriminatory practice policy and action plan is a useful way to keep the issue in a central position and can support your efforts to implement it.
- Ensuring your agency has representatives from disadvantaged groups on its management committee and employs staff from such groups. The existence and operation of an equal opportunities policy will be important in this respect.
- Through a range of measures making the living with teenagers groups you run accessible and relevant to people from disadvantaged groups. These measures can include translations of material, co-working with workers from disadvantaged groups and using appropriate, attractive publicity.

Monitoring, evaluating and being critical of your practice

There are several steps that can be taken to improve your practice when running living with teenagers groups:

- Use feedback from the parents' evaluation forms received at the end of groups to look at the range of ways that your anti-discriminatory practice can be improved.
- If your agency has an action plan for its anti-discriminatory practice policy the plan, if stated in measurable terms, can be reviewed regularly by your management committee, managers, team or colleagues. These reviews can then be used to look at ways in which practice can be improved and progress monitored.

A case study

Putting the theoretical ideas referred to earlier in this chapter into practice is a challenge. It is particularly helpful to think of applying theory to practice as a *process* Equally important, it is also essential to see the process as a *continuing* and *central* activity in your work. In this case study we share our learning and mistakes so that we can help you move forward in the process of anti-discriminatory practice.

Fun and families groups for Asian parents

When the Centre was formed in 1990 the staff had no experience of running groups other than for white parents in predominantly rural areas. During 1991 and 1992 attempts were made to generate an interest in running 'fun and families' groups in the City of Leicester. This was because the Centre staff wanted to make their services available to parents in all areas as part of their anti-discriminatory practice policy.

Contacts with several African-Caribbean parents led us to approach two family centres who had significant proportions of black parents in attendance. However, no success was achieved in the idea of running a 'fun and families' group for black parents. With hindsight there were three main stumbling blocks to our efforts:

we did not employ or work with black staff, all the staff were white and male and we did not have a written anti-discriminatory practice policy.

During late 1992 we renewed our efforts to try to overcome the stumbling blocks to running fun and families groups with black parents. At this time an Asian social work student joined the Centre for a placement. With the student's great energy and enthusiasm a venue was found in the community wing of a local school attended by 95% of Asian pupils. In addition a partnership with an Asian health visitor was developed, and the school community tutor agreed to publicise the group. In order to try to promote attendance the student, the health visitor and a member of the Centre staff undertook a display at the school.

In early 1993 a 'fun and families' group, co-led by the student, a health visitor and a member of the Centre staff, was successfully run and attended initially by eight parents, reducing to five by the end of the seven-week programme. From this experience we learned there was a need for good, properly typed translations of our material, handouts, into Gujarati and that this was going to be essential for future groups. In addition, the fact that the member of the Centre staff had attended an evening class to learn conversational Gujarati had proved to be very useful in two respects. It helped him to understand when parts of the sessions were conducted in Gujarati. Particularly, though, it gave him a much better understanding of the culture and customs associated with the language.

Trying to persuade Asian parents to attend groups seemed to be quite difficult. Apart from a general reluctance to attend groups and the possibility of previous negative experiences of white professionals, there seemed to be two cultural factors at work. First, the belief that parents, and specifically the mother was 'to blame' for child behaviour difficulties, or the feeling that the child's behaviour reflected on the parents, seemed to be very strong disincentives to attend groups. Second, there seemed to be a reluctance to admit to child behaviour difficulties. The parents themselves gave one particular reason for this: it was that the marriage chances of female children were thought to be reduced if they gained a reputation for behaviour difficulties.

No male parents attended. This seemed to be because of the expectation that child care was female responsibility and it was more pronounced within Asian families than we had expected.

The parents who did attend the group evaluated the outcome as positively as white parents who had attended previous groups. However, some parts of the group programme seemed to be more or less effective. For example, the exercises on defining behaviour seemed to be very readily grasped by the parents. This seemed to be related to the nature of Gujarati as a language. Unlike English, the verb is always at the end of the sentence and the sort of vague words for behaviour – for example, naughty, disobedient and so on – that are common in English, are not used. Another example occurred in the third session on the use of praise. This session, and in particular the use of 'Fun Stickers', seemed to be extremely effective. It appeared that this was because Gujarati does not make much use of the equivalent of 'please' and 'thank you' but uses 'respectful speech'. Therefore the use of praise, hugs, cuddles and associated Fun Stickers was found to be very effective.

In autumn 1993 and spring 1994, two further groups were run for Asian parents in the same school. The first was run with the Asian health visitor, another female Asian student and a white male Centre worker. The second was run with an Asian community worker, a male Asian student and a white male Centre worker. Both were successful, but initial numbers and dwindling attendance were a cause of concern.

During the second group the Asian community worker tried to increase the numbers after the first session by giving a talk to a group of Asian parents who were completing a Pre-school Playgroups course on childcare. Amazingly, 26 parents attended the next session! In subsequent weeks the group settled down to about 14/15 parents. In addition, because many of the parents viewed the group as a course, presenting them with a certificate at the end of the group proved to be extremely popular. Since then groups at the school have been run on a regular basis, attracting 14 to 15 parents per group, and attendance throughout has been good.

Living with teenagers groups for Asian parents

Following the success of the fun and families group programmes, a pilot group was run for Asian fathers of teenagers in January/February 1996. Seven fathers attended this group and the evaluation of the group showed that it was regarded as successful and helpful by the parents that attended. A follow-up evaluation was done six months after the group by a Diploma in Social Work student, Trevor Collumbell, and the details of his findings are referred to in Chapter 13.

Key to success

The key to success in the Centre's work with Asian parents seems to be to offer the following:

- The group appears more attractive to Asian parents if presented as an 'advanced care course' rather than as a 'group for parents with child behaviour difficulties'. The parents prefer to elect to come without being pressured. However, the Asian community tutor is able to offer the group to parents who are known to be having difficulties with their children or teenager's behaviour, and have sought advice.
- The Centre now has almost all its written material and handouts translated into Gujarati and Urdu. In addition, because of the partnership with Asian community workers we are able to conduct groups in Gujarati, Urdu and English.
- The venues where groups are run have professionally run crèches.
- The Asian community worker's links within the local community are

very positive and 'word of mouth' publicity for the groups is, as always, very effective. In addition, their knowledge of cultural and religious beliefs allows the material to be made relevant to Gujarati-speaking Hindus or Urdu-speaking Moslems. This also allows basic planning errors to be avoided. For example, a group in the Belgrave area would not run during 'Diwali' in October/November – the Hindu equivalent of Christmas/New Year.

● Our knowledge of local Asian communities will be enhanced by the appointment of Rita Naag, an Asian social worker, who joined the Centre staff in early 1998.

Living with teenagers groups for African-Caribbean parents

The Centre staff have been consulting with a range of African-Caribbean professional staff in a variety of statutory and voluntary agencies to obtain opinions about changes to the living with teenagers programme to make it as relevant as possible to African-Caribbean parents. In addition, we have been seeking a partnership with individuals and/or agencies who would be interested in running a living with teenagers group in Leicester for African-Caribbean parents. The response has been very positive and we are hoping to be able to run our first group of this nature in 1998.

Future developments

The important lessons we have learnt in running groups in a variety of settings and for people of different races, genders, cultures and religions is that such groups will work as long as the leaders have:

● A good, detailed knowledge of the language, culture, religious beliefs and child-rearing practices of the people attending.
● The group leaders are representative of the local population and there is a balance of black/white and female/male co-leaders.
● The co-leaders are able to be flexible in materials used (ie. handouts, exercises and video material) in order to respect the culture, gender and religious beliefs of all those attending the groups.

The Moyenda Project was set up in 1991 to research the support needs of black families and to begin the process of developing an appropriate, culturally sensitive model for working with black families in the United Kingdom. The Project Report (June 1995) suggests that key elements for a better response to the needs of black parents include:

- Services need to be more culturally sensitive and, in particular, need to recognise the differences between the experiences of black and white parents.
- Services should have a positive black identity through the appointment of black team leaders and culturally representative teams.
- Developing links with community groups is important so that black parents have easy access to culturally appropriate information on parenting and parent support groups.
- Family support professionals should undergo regular anti-racism and cultural sensitivity training.

Whereas Centre staff and associated co-leaders have experience of running groups for Asian parents – specifically for Gujarati-speaking Hindus and Urdu-speaking Moslems – we are aware that we have no direct experience of running groups for African-Caribbean parents or Asian parents of other languages (e.g. Punjabi or Bengali) or religions. We would view the development of such groups as an urgent priority, and also as part of the 'process' of the 'continuing' activity of anti-discriminatory practice.

4   Social learning theory

Applying the principles of basic social learning theory

Everybody, consciously or otherwise, continually shapes and changes each other's behaviour. Social learning theory (SLT) has examined that process and can provide guidelines to direct efforts to change behaviour deliberately and effectively.

SLT provides us with a greater choice and level of control over our affairs. It enables people to recognise the way other people influence them. Then, if they have some objection, the knowledge provides a way of countering such control. The theory is scientific and like the theory of gravity it applies universally without bias or prejudice regarding race, gender or disability. Because it always considers the context in which behaviour occurs, it avoids labelling anybody as 'a problem'. It provides simply a means of identifying behaviours and the way they are maintained. Whoever uses these ideas to deliberately change behaviour should think carefully before taking action simply because the techniques are so effective. Three checks at least would be advisable:

- Is the behaviour part of the target person's 'normal' development or a justifiable reaction to events?
- Is it ethical to work for the proposed change?
- Are the family feeling pressured by relatives or statutory agencies to demand conformity without understanding the possible consequences?

Although the theory itself may be free from bias or prejudice, people who work with and in families are not. It is therefore vitally important that

45

workers do not make assumptions about the values and methods of managing behaviours used by families of different races and cultures. Nor should they make assumptions about the roles young people may be expected to play within their families.

The ethical application of the theory must rest with the practitioners and the families. This is because, just as with any effective theory, it can be used for good or ill. Consequently, the care with which it is used is all the more important and the responsibility upon those using it is so much greater.

The basic principles of social learning theory

In practical terms SLT proposes that 'behaviour' is learned. It can therefore always be unlearned! Or an alternative can be learned to replace a behaviour judged to be unacceptable.

This brings a new perspective to many seemingly intractable and impossibly chaotic situations. The model simplifies intervention by providing just two alternatives:

1   It can identify behaviour which is not occurring as frequently as desired. Technically, this would be a behaviour 'deficit'. An example might be that a depressed young person is not getting enough exercise. Well-tested principles and techniques can then be used to 'increase' the level of exercise. We can therefore increase behaviour which is not occurring frequently enough.

2   Alternatively, a behaviour may be performed 'in excess', occurring very often. This at times might be considered undesirable. A great many teenagers rebel against convention at some stage. Sometimes the manner in which they do that can become a grave social disadvantage. Learning how to control themselves and get their view across without totally alienating others or resorting to deliberate antagonism is an essential social skill. Well-tested principles and techniques are available which can be used to decrease behaviour which happens too often.

The assessment

The following steps offer a structured model about what to do and how to do it when applying the theory, and also indicate why the methodology is so effective:

Step 1: describe the behaviour

First of all the behaviour must be precisely described: terms like he is 'rebellious' or she is 'moody' are unhelpful. If we stop to think about such terms, each can embrace many behaviours. For example, rebellious might include drinking, taking drugs, swearing, coming in late or not getting up in the morning. Moody might include not talking, not listening, being upset, crying or storming out of the room.

The skill of careful description is most important. Often it is the case, as with the examples above, that one behaviour leads to another. By dealing with one low-key behaviour, other more stressful ones are nipped in the bud and prevented from becoming problems.

During our living with teenagers groups, parents do exercises in defining a behaviour they find difficulties with and want to change. They then check out with other parents in the group if their description of the behaviour is clear. Provided everyone has the same perception, the actual words used are not so important. Once clear descriptions are agreed, it is probably sensible to choose just one or two behaviours to work with at first. This may seem as if the 'real problem' is being overlooked or trivialised. That is not the case. Serious violence has been overcome by simply ensuring some positive communication with the young person involved has been established. This demonstrates how selecting a simple task can resolve a really complex problem!

It is important for parents to choose target behaviours with care and really commit themselves to the task, as it is easy to get distracted or let initial commitment falter. If parents have chosen well, and work at applying SLT precisely, there is every reason to believe some change can be achieved. One success leads to another and, if more work needs doing, this will give confidence and enthusiasm to tackle further work.

Step 2: 'track' the behaviour

Studies have shown that 'tracking' behaviour is a crucial skill. In the everyday hurly-burly of life, many behaviours go unnoticed or are responded to inconsistently. For example, sometimes smoking will attract encouragement or chastisement in the same home by the same people. Doing something about it requires that these differing responses are noted and the time or context of the variations noticed. It has been found that people who learn to 'track' problem behaviours quickly resolve the difficulties they are experiencing (Paterson, 1974).

A way of tracking behaviour is to keep written records and charts. This makes the process so much easier in a number of ways and also enables progress to be monitored with greater accuracy. They can be used in two important ways:

1   Therapeutically, it can be extremely important to demonstrate progress is being achieved. Often those involved are too fraught to notice or feel the difference when initial small improvements occur. Therefore, charts and records actively demonstrate that progress is in fact happening.
2   Ethically, the adviser needs to realise how things are moving so that fine tuning or changes to suggested programmes can be made.

Once records are kept, even for a short time, they often show that the behaviour to be changed is mainly confined to a given time or situation. For example, this can be at key points during the day such as getting up or washing or coming in on time! Finding out this type of information can help to concentrate efforts to change to a specific time-limited period. A parent might then, for example, decide to try and influence the behaviour of staying out late. Thus the task is made less onerous for parents by narrowing it down to specific times and behaviours.

Another advantage of keeping records is that this can assist the learning process and consequent changes in behaviour. An example of this was seen in the case of a teenager who was embarrassed by wetting the bed. He was asked to keep his own records in order to check them against the ones his mother kept. It was demonstrated that she had exaggerated the problem. He then took charge and the problem was quickly owned by him and reduced even further.

If you have the equipment and feel comfortable with the idea, making audio or video recordings of behaviour can also be another very useful way of making records. Young people respond well to seeing or hearing what they are really like! Quite often, it comes as a real shock to watch themselves communicating with their parents. A typical comment has been 'Did I really speak like that'? Similarly, parents can also learn a thing or two about their own communication and responses! Video and tape recording, when used appropriately, does work much more effectively with young people. It is more successful than their feeling 'lectured' to by their parents.

Discovering the context of the behaviour

The next stage is to discover the context in which the difficult or problematic behaviour occurs. It is so important at this stage to take time and effort over this part of the assessment. Standing back and carefully collecting as much detail about *what* is actually happening will be helpful as the assessment develops. It is all too easy and natural to rush ahead and make false assumptions about *why* it is happening. These are often inaccurate and unhelpful because they speculate and infer other peoples' intentions without checking the evidence for those views.

Step 1: identify the 'trigger'

Look for antecedents or triggers. These are events which come immediately before the selected behaviour. It is necessary to find out where, when, frequency and who is present at the time. These events are probably the stimuli to which the behaviour is a response. Stimuli are most significant in maintaining current behaviour. They provide an environment capable of suggesting, encouraging, instructing and offering ideas which can be copied or acted upon. Generally speaking, people love to copy. Modelling and copying behaviour provides a setting to show how something might be done and provides an opportunity to practice it. It may also suggest or prompt an action, causing it to be repeated. For example, even shy young people begin to copy the fashions they see in magazines and imitate from their peers. They start to give quite different meanings to words from those assumed by their parents. The environment encourages behaviours by giving examples, opportunities and prompts. Adjusting to the resulting behaviour can have a profound effect upon a whole family.

Step 2: observe the behaviour

Examine the selected behaviour and the relationship it has to the events which immediately precede it. If you strengthen or enhance the stimuli, you increase the behaviour. If you weaken or modify the stimuli, you decrease the behaviour.

Step 3: note what follows the behaviour

Note the consequences or events which immediately follow the behaviour. Reinforcers, sometimes loosely referred to as 'pay offs', are events which occur after the behaviour. During observation, you will soon notice how a young person will be encouraged by the response he or she receives. An example might be a teenager coming home with their first earring, or tattoo. If it was an act of bravado, and is met with shocked horror, it will have achieved its purpose; the behaviour will have been positively reinforced.

If a behaviour is performed infrequently or is non-existent, it has probably been 'punished'. If that is the case, the task is to identify those factors which are aversive or inhibiting the behaviour. These can usually be observed but may appear contradictory. For example, some people find being the focus of attention or receiving hugs discomforting. They may then seek to avoid attracting such seemingly desirable action by decreasing behaviour which may invite such responses. By definition, if a behaviour exists and is performed frequently, it is being reinforced. SLT assessment involves carefully seeking out facets in the interactions between parent and teenager which sustain or reward the behaviour.

The ABC letters refer to the words listed below.

Antecedent ➤ Behaviour ➤ Consequences

If this is undertaken thoroughly, it provides a very good understanding of what maintains one behaviour and reduces another. This is commonly to do with the way people interact with each other.

As young people mature, we sometimes find that the observed visual ABCs do not provide an adequate explanation for the behaviour we want to address. The model may then need elaborating.

The significant antecedents may include quite distant historical facts. For example, in an extreme situation, one foster child struggled and fought to avoid bathing. No progress could be made until the information came to hand that she had been abused in the bath. The puzzling behaviour seemed to come out of the blue but was in fact triggered by a powerful memory. It had been stored in the young person's memory and was therefore not obvious to her adult carers. Such an example highlights the care we need to take to ensure we speak to young people and try to understand the meaning of, and their reasons behind, their behaviour. So, in working with teenagers, it is necessary to consider extra components and an elaboration of the model.

Antecedent ➤ (thoughts)──➤Behaviour ➤ (feelings)──➤Consequences

It is evident that there are thoughts in teenagers' heads which cannot be seen or observed, but which have a very strong influence on behaviour. The young person referred to above is one example of the way in which very strong feelings (i.e. experience of sexual abuse) can trigger particular behaviour (i.e. refusal to have a bath). Equally, in between behaviour and the pay-off or consequence, a young person's feelings may lead to a behaviour not being repeated. For example, a young person may feel that a parent is not going to listen. If the teenager tries to talk to the parent, and only receives a cursory or lukewarm response, they may, because of their existing feelings, see this is a negative response (i.e. not a pay-off) and therefore not try again. This is even more likely to happen if other complex feelings, such as the fact that the parent is a step- or adoptive parent, are in evidence. In Chapter 6 the relationship between thoughts, feelings and behaviour is examined more closely.

Making plans for improvement

Step 1: be positive

Whenever possible, be positive. For example, rewarding a teenager for coming in early or on time, rather than having punishments for coming in late, is likely to work better. Another example might be that of rewarding loving or kind statements rather than trying to stop jealous and hurtful ones. It is more enjoyable to administer and receive positive approaches, and it has been found in practice that other behaviours will also change without additional work. This is probably because the joy of success encourages other improvements. It has also been found that the improvements hold up longer over time when they are achieved through positive means. Finally, punishments may have undesirable side effects in the form of further rebellion!

Step 2: have a clear goal

Be clear and single minded, and know what you want to achieve. Remember that, with SLT, you can either *increase* behaviour or *decrease* behaviour.

Do not get sidetracked into looking for more involved explanations. Hold firm to the practical fact that often, by changing one or two behaviours, wider benefits are achieved. To do this, you must focus on changing the selected target behaviour. This will be a demanding enough task in itself to achieve. An example here might be when a parent complains that her daughter's bedroom is an 'untidy tip'. With a teenager it might be necessary to enter into negotiations and move towards the target in small steps. Putting dirty washing in the clothes basket could be a start (reward = praise + new clothing), or clearing a space for a new poster (reward = positive attention + new poster). Then an imaginative and enjoyable programme can be worked out that is rewarding for the child and parent. With teenagers and older children, it is almost certain that some compromise will be an essential part of a successful outcome.

Step 3: use punishment as a last resort

If some negative or troublesome behaviours do not respond to the positive methods, punishing techniques can be used with caution. The problem, however, is that they have the potential to backfire. For example, physical punishment has a law of diminishing returns and quite quickly teaches the recipient to avoid getting caught rather than to amend their ways. Teenagers are likely to harbour a huge sense of unfairness at such treatment.

Relationships can quickly break down and the parent becomes more and more desperate. Indeed, increased family violence is often the unintended result of physical punishment. For example, a parent in a group lost his temper and pushed his son into his bedroom. The son then hit him with a golf club!

Even those techniques used for reducing behaviour which are less upsetting do not teach what you do want to happen. Therefore a kind of vacuum is created because neither young person nor parents are clear about what they do want.

It is probably best to use 'punishing' techniques only as a last resort and always together with other 'positive' strategies. This cannot be overstressed. Quite often, once parents get into 'punishing' techniques, the more positive strategies are just lost and forgotten about. It is very important to try to create a benign and positive package of change strategies.

Tools of the trade: ways of changing behaviour

There are some books (Gambrill, 1977, Herbert, 1978) which contain a comprehensive range of available techniques. By using more than one reference book, you can get an overall view and avoid what can often be a 'cook book' approach. Having a range of options is essential, and their use can only be accurate if the assessment is carefully undertaken.

Each technique has a specific purpose. For example, the technique of planned ignoring is effective for extreme attention-seeking behaviour, whereas 'overlearning' is more effective in dealing with avoidance behaviours. A young person might provoke an argument to get attention, or use exactly the same ploy to create a diversion, as a way of avoiding an unpleasant task such as having to tidy up.

The assessment defines, selects and tries to understand the sense of the individual problematic behaviour. The task of the worker is to help parents identify the most effective strategies which they feel comfortable using, based upon the parents' own assessment of what behaviour to tackle and why it is happening.

When trying to increase behaviour, ensure that the child or young person knows exactly what is expected of him or her. This can involve far more than we think at first sight. We must not assume they know what is expected or that they can actually do the task. Therefore, a successful change plan will include:

1   Clear guidelines which are fully understood by and acceptable to all concerned.

2 Modelling the task to ensure that parents have the skills needed to achieve what is required. This may require role play, practising and correcting minor errors and checking to ensure the young person has some incentive and commitment to accomplish the task.

3 It is important to reinforce or reward the achievement of small steps or approximations. This could be, for example, agreeing to start homework at a certain time; the next step could be to work for half an hour before a break. Then gradually increase the comprehensiveness of the task until the goal is achieved. Every individual step should be rewarded.

Effective reinforcers

The most effective forms of reinforcers are:

- Social rewards such as smiles, 'well done', praise and physical contact – these are the most powerful and long-lasting, even if some teenagers seem reluctant to receive them.
- Social activities or shared outings or games – these all facilitate good communication between the generations.
- Money and goodies are the least effective reinforcers although, used in conjunction with the above, they can add variety and a sense of genuine achievement when used imaginatively.

It needs to be stressed here that the above three points are generalised statements and care needs to be taken that due consideration, respect and thought is given to the family's race, culture and religious needs. It is also worth bearing in mind a young person's history.

Effective forms of decreasing behaviour

Reinforce an alternative behaviour

This is the most powerful method. Parents often come to a group wanting to decrease a behaviour about which they are very concerned, for example setting fire to the carpet or throwing knives. Obviously, these are serious problems and parents will be worried! By choosing an alternative behaviour to work on we avoid the focus of attention all going towards the matches or knives. If the targeted behaviour was 'to reduce Dean's knife-throwing', then the whole idea of knife-throwing is still the main focus. Alternatively, if the targeted behaviour chosen was 'for Dean to talk with mother and father for two minutes or more each day', then it can be seen that the focus is turned away from assaulting and damaging to something constructive and pleasurable for both parties. At times it may need persuasion to convince parents and carers enough to agree to something which feels like rewarding someone for being 'bad'! What should be stressed is that we are rewarding specific behaviour, rather than the individual as a person.

Ignoring

This can also be very powerful but sometimes tricky to achieve, as often problems arise when good behaviour is ignored unintentionally. An almost ritual regime may need to be used for a while to establish a changed pattern of responses, for example, deliberately turning away dramatically, turning your back on the young person, refusing to be drawn into an argument and walking firmly from the scene. For some very destructive behaviour this technique is only advisable if a partner or friend is around to make sure there is no risk to the young person or property.

Withdrawing benefits or privileges

This technique is where items such as pocket money, outings or stopping out late are removed. The teenager needs to be fully aware of what is to be removed and why it is being removed. It is only then that he or she can take responsibility for their action. Like all of these more 'punishing' techniques, they are open to misuse. For example, it can be easy to remove the whole week's pocket money, stop the outing which all the family has been looking forward to, or lock the new bicycle away in the shed for a month. The young person then has nothing to work towards with such punishments and may therefore 'give up'. The best policy is to remove only a small part of the benefit or privilege.

Response cost

This technique can be used to show that there is a *cost* to undesirable behaviour. It places responsibility for some unpleasant consequences firmly upon the young person's own shoulders.

Tokens can be given for meeting expected targets and bonus tokens for performing the tasks on time, for example. The bonuses can then be removed if predetermined, unacceptable behaviour occurs. This teaches that individual performance can earn both advantages and penalties. When removing tokens, it is important that only bonus tokens are removed as penalties. It is very important that too much should not be lost too easily. If all of a young person's pocket money is removed he or she has nothing to work towards. When young people are in no-win situations they can become unpredictable and negative. There is a detailed description of this technique in the programme outline for Session 5.

Reinforcement schedules

These are simply lists of potentially interesting items such as music, food, smoking, sex, reading and so on. The young person is asked, in a playful way, to rate each item on a scale of 1–5 (1 = do not like, 5 = like very much). Using such a questionnaire is a means of discovering in more detail which things a young person likes. Some of these may be used as ways of encouraging acceptable behaviour, although only if it was felt in the teenager's best interests to do so. The value of the schedule is to encourage communication and interaction between the parents and teenager as much as to find useful pay-offs to promote acceptable behaviour. (See Session 3 of the programme outline for further details.)

Finally, always encourage parents to keep records throughout the entire intervention. It is worth the effort even if it seems like an extra chore. It makes it possible to take responsibility for what change is being achieved, which can be comforting and reassuring to people. Quite often they appreciate the integrity and attention to detail. Records also indicate when to change an intervention which is not working well.

A further reason for keeping records is that, initially, an attempt to change a behaviour can, for perhaps several days, lead to only small decreases in the behaviour. Such small improvements could be overlooked and lost without records. Without accurate records, a parent may, after two or three days of trying a new approach with no apparent success, conclude that the strategy does not work. In addition, keeping records takes the mystique out of the relationship between parents and the worker. It puts the information and power in their own hands and avoids unnecessary feelings of dependency.

5 Resolving family conflict

There are many different ways of trying to resolve family conflict. Work can be done with the whole family, or with individual young people, or parents, or various combinations of these. The report, *Focus on Teenagers*, published by the Department of Health (1996), offers comprehensive lists of projects.

Theoretical base for resolving family conflict

Our work has developed from working with parents in groups which do not include the young people. We offer a seven-week course. It is necessary therefore to select with some care exercises and skills which parents will find most useful. In this chapter the theoretical base of our work is examined, along with the options for exercises, which parents experiencing conflict may try out in their efforts to resolve the differences they may have with their teenagers.

The basic ideas from social learning used in the fun and family groups still apply, but there are significant differences in application. Teenagers test out possible levels of independence. So although parents need to be consistent in their own standards, they cannot impose them upon developing offspring. The ethos of the teenager groups is therefore much more to do with negotiation and influence rather than control.

Sharon Foster led a workshop in the 1980s which identified from shared research that most family conflict was based upon verbal arguments about specific issues. It noted that poor resolution of the conflicts had one or a combination of the following skill deficits:

- Poor communication skills
- Distorted cognitions relating to family functioning
- Poor problem-solving skills.

The selection of target behaviours when addressing these difficulties is a fairly exacting task. The underlying principal is that some behaviours are exhibited too often (i.e., they are in excess) and other behaviours do not happen often enough (i.e., they are in deficit).

Poor communication skills

Poor communication skills are characterised by one or more of the following:

- Raised voices (too much shouting)
- Accusations rather than focus on the complaint
- Going off the point
- Use of more and more words to win an argument.

These are excessive behaviours which aggravate rather than solve conflicts. As such, reducing their use is helpful. One of the consequences of behaviour like this is that behaviours which could be helpful – for example 'listening' or 'asking without demanding' – disappear or are neglected. Increasing such deficit behaviours is the most effective way to resolve disputes. It also reduces the excessive behaviours.

Listening

Listening is by far and away the most important skill and the one that predominantly gets lost when there is conflict. Foster (1985) cited research indicating that, from a sample of interventions, the most common targets in percentage terms were as follows:

Excess/Deficit	Intervention	Target percentage
Deficit	Listening	68.4%
Excess	Increase in speaking	42.1%
Excess	Accusations	36.8%
Deficit	Staying on the topic	36.5%

We know that to increase behaviour certain things need to occur. Applying this to 'listening' using the ABC model, outlined in Chapter 4, we find:

Antecedents	Behaviour	Consequences
Give information about Demonstrate skills involved in Devise an exercise and give clear instructions Ensure these can be practised	LISTENING	Offer positive feedback Offer constructive criticism Give genuine encouragement and praise when listening happens

There is important information about listening, which needs to be shared:

- It involves more than hearing the words. Part of the skill of listening is to be able to detect the feelings which lie beneath the words. Someone might well say, 'Oh that's all right', but in fact be feeling very hurt and let down. It is far from easy to pick up such nuances and it is not surprising that often people are misunderstood.
- It requires the speaker to receive feedback to know they have been understood and that the listener has accurately followed the jist of what was said. So listening effectively may involve checking out that the speaker has been genuinely heard and understood: 'Have I got this right – you can live with the fact that the date is cancelled, but you feel very disappointed?' If a person is to feel listened to they need evidence that you have heard them accurately and have taken notice of what they say.
- Listening requires time and it is important that the listener holds back from their own agenda so that the listener knows their meaning has been digested. Apart from checking with them that you hear the words, sometimes a space – silence – is needed just to establish that you are taking it in. Try not to react too quickly, or plunge into your own agenda before the implications of their words have sunk in.
- It requires appropriate body language, for example, good eye contact, relaxed open gestures and all the non-verbal cues from body posture and expression which can enhance or defeat attempts to communicate.

In effect, this is using the core counselling conditions of empathy, acceptance and congruence (Rogers, 1977), without which any techniques or responses have been shown to be less effective, if not even damaging.

We invite parents to practice this complex cluster of skills in a role play. The way this is used in the programme is described in Chapter 9, Session 4. First they are asked to enact an argument, perhaps a scene in which conflict breaks out when a young person comes in very late. The mother is distraught with worry and the father angry at the lack of consideration shown by the young person. With a shy group the leaders can role-play the parents. The most effective way is to do this badly enough so all the features of poor communication are demonstrated. This will include: people not listening to each other, volume increasing, going off the point, saying hurtful things to each other. The scene is then repeated, but this time the following ground rules are kept:

- Each person has a turn to speak.
- Everybody else listens to what they say.
- The listeners encourage the speaker with non-verbal signs – eye contact, encouraging grunts, etc.
- They must only speak to check that they have heard correctly.
- They leave sufficient silence to enable the speaker to know his or her words have been noted.
- Only then does the next person begin.

Everybody will have a chance to speak. They are directed not to speak for others but to offer their own view and include how they feel about things. When each has spoken and been listened to, each can speak a second time to respond to other peoples' comments. In spite of it being rather artificial, people find it exceedingly difficult not to get drawn into arguments or to avoid being dominated by their own agenda of solutions or points to be made. Very experienced communicators and workers have commented after this experience on how much it has shown them. They have realised how superficial the attention given routinely to other people is, and how difficult it can be to listen really effectively.

Making effective requests

'Making effective requests' or 'asking without demanding' can be similarly examined. If we want to get a point across powerfully the basic model can help in formulating a plan.

Antecedents	Behaviour	Consequences
Think carefully about the message you wish to convey Set reasonable expectations Pre-plan words, tone, body language, emotional content – practice saying it as planned Try it out!	Inviting someone to share a discussion about a family outing	They listen They object Negotiations start

Try to be clear about your objective and indicators of success. An objection may not sound like encouragement or reinforcement, but if the objective, as in the example above, was to promote discussion, then it succeeded!

It can be seen that this involves a range of quite complicated and coordinated skills. Body postures must match the messages given if confusion is to be avoided. Non-verbal signals include emotional cues: in our work we find over and again that young people feel unloved, even hated, by their parents and carers. It can come as a surprise for them to hear that the 'telling off' had its roots in genuine concern for their well-being. So often the element of expressing emotion is neglected until it has become anger or so hurtful that it is aggressively expressed.

A way of dealing with this confusion is first to express positive emotion: 'I would like you to come in on time because I am worried sick that you may be mugged.' It is important, of course, to ensure that the exercises relate to whoever uses them in a realistic way. This can be very disarming if someone is cross and expecting criticism. It is also important to own and express individual negative emotion. People can suffer in silence and then explode. If that happens, recipients can feel attacked or accused in a very hurtful way. 'You make me sick' has the potential to be a very undermining statement and one likely to provoke an antagonistic response. 'I feel sick when you do that' owns the feeling and is more likely to make someone reconsider their actions than an accusation and placing of blame would. If feelings can be expressed near to the event, they come out more powerfully and effectively. In one case a sister was able to express how upset and undermined she felt by her brother's constant teasing. He went very quiet when it dawned on him that 'having a bit of macho fun' could be so hurtful to her.

The meaning of gestures can vary depending upon the culture. For example, eye contact is seen as respectful and encouraging in some cultures, but as offensive in others. For some a big hug would be a sign of warmth and encouragement, for others it would be intrusive and embarrassing. Care therefore needs to be taken to match sound and action, together with a humble appreciation that it is possible that genuine attempts to share ideas can be misunderstood when couched in terms not easily accepted by others.

It is also the case that if genuine attempts to communicate are met with disinterest or antagonism, good intentions can easily evaporate. Conversation which starts to placate or reason things out can be responded to by body language which says stay away. An argument can then develop as a natural reaction to being misunderstood. It is possible of course that the person is expecting criticism and disapproval and their action is intended to defend themselves against attack.

These observations seem so obvious and straightforward when we read about them. However, in actual practice, there are traps into which everybody falls from time to time. One way of overcoming such traps is to give some thought to the selection of words and practise various alternatives as 'dry runs' before the actual conversation takes place. In groups we ask parents to practise these aspects of making requests through a role play described in Chapter 9 Session 4 using a scene relating to 'putting clothes away'. This has the advantage of getting a variety of useful and supportive feedback. One of the most common points that is learnt from this exercise is that, without realising it, many parents have used shouting at their teenagers as a means of getting things done. Sadly, it has often become a habit, and a very ineffective one.

Other areas to practise could be: giving encouraging messages and receiving nice messages. People can be embarrassed when praised or sometimes suspect the motive of the person offering pleasant personal comment – 'I wonder what they are after?' They then respond in a manner that discourages future compliments. Difficulties can be experienced when giving or receiving difficult messages. It can feel even more fraught to present critical opinion or expressions of displeasure in a balanced and positive fashion. If emotions are running high any request can be misconstrued. 'Please tidy your bedroom' can become interpreted as 'I'm a useless, unacceptable individual'.

For these reasons it is worth encouraging the practice and getting personal experience of these communication skills, as well as using them on others. Try to experience receiving compliments and check your reactions. Also check personal individual reactions to critical comment. In this way a more rounded awareness of personal interactions is achieved.

These basic areas of communication, once understood and practised to a 'good enough' standard, lay a good foundation for moving on to problem resolution.

Distorted cognitions relating to family functions

In the groups we use a role play about coming in late: this illustrates the way cognitions can become distorted. The young person will often end up thinking they are rejected, that their parents do not like them but are simply seeking to restrict their activities from a purely controlling perspective. If they think this then they are likely to respond in a negative way to their parents. It is also possible for the parents to begin to believe that the only sense in the young person's behaviour is to 'get at them and hurt them'. If they think behaviour signifies deliberate attempts to hurt them they also will respond to their teenagers in a negative way.

Distorted cognitions are dealt with in more depth in Chapter 6, but it may be helpful to consider them from the simple perspective of behaviours which either occur too often or not often enough.

When someone expects to be hurt or criticised it is likely that they will develop the habit of defending themselves, often by going on the attack. In the role play a young person taken to task for being late usually gets very angry while the parents also have had stress to deal with. The following ABC illustrates this.

Antecedents	Behaviour	Consequences
Long period of waiting Anxious parent convinced teenager deliberately trying to upset them Worried young person expecting to be punished	Coming in very late	Fierce argument Everyone feels hurt and acts and speaks unreasonably

The distorted cognitions based on inaccurate information in this scenario contribute to a conflict. The young person was missing how worried the parent was, and the parent was missing how fearful the teenager was.

Poor problem-solving skills

Conflict arises when specific behaviours, including ways of speaking and moods, occur too often or not enough. The essence of problem-solving is to generate alternatives and select mutually accepted options. There is not time within the programme to use exercises to demonstrate every step of problem-solving, but during the second half of each session, as parents shape up their home tasks, the various steps could be introduced informally, perhaps even used as separate tasks in the week ahead. Poor-problem solving is marked by a paucity of alternatives, too few options and too little evaluation and negotiation. This deficit in ideas and speaking together constructively produces a rigid and limited frame of reference to work with and can result in guessing what others think rather than checking. That leads to misunderstanding. It could also be the case that too many ideas, and too much discussion, would prevent a plan for change coming to fruition. This produces frustration and a lack of satisfying social interaction.

A sequence or model which counteracts the stultifying effects of these extremes is available. The emphasis can be placed where it is most appropriate, either to increase the range of options, or to decrease prevarication and avoidance of taking active steps to resolve matters.

Brainstorming

A useful first step is to play a nonsense game in which everyone without thinking shouts out, or writes down, possible solutions to the dilemmas they are facing. Obviously there will be some fantasy, foolish items – emigrate to a desert island or win the lottery – amongst the ideas thought of in this way. The more ideas generated the better, as this is intended to increase imaginative thinking.

Negotiate and compromise

The second step is to negotiate and compromise so that, after perhaps sharing a laugh, the nonsense can be discarded from the list – the desert island may be nice but it is totally impractical! Some items will also be put to one side if they seem not to be practical or mutually acceptable at that moment in time. The task is to select two or three practical and possible solutions which each person feels might work. Each member of the family needs to express their view about reasonable suggestions. Coming in early may alleviate a mother's anxiety but it could also ruin a young person's social life, so compromise and understanding of each other begins. Probably neither wants to hurt the other, so they have to find a way of reassuring each other without riding roughshod over the other's feelings or imposing debilitating restrictions upon their activities. The exercise could produce a list of each person's needs as follows:

Dad wants	Young person wants	Mum wants
Less arguing	Mum to be less protective	More control
Peace		Family together more
Young person to be tidier	Less nagging from Dad	
	Less hassle	
Young person in on time	Later nights outs	
Not to be used for telling young person off so much	More freedom	

There are some well-tested guidelines to help in selecting a workable target:

- Choose observable tasks. For example, 'more freedom' is too vague to check out and misunderstandings are bound to arise. Being in by 11pm would be a more specific and promising aim to work towards. It would give mum more control and reduce the number of occasions that dad had to 'tell off' the teenager, and it would give the youngster more freedom and less hassle.
- Be as specific as possible, but also set achievable goals. Agree to compromise – coming in early for three nights each week is more achievable than having a curfew for all occasions!
- Don't be too ambitious The final goal may be large: the family more together ... peace ... less hassle, but break the process of getting there down into manageable steps. Deal with coming in late, then move on to time together, and so on.

The action plan

The third step is to devise an action plan to which everybody has contributed and has some commitment. It can be useful to write that plan down and have everybody sign it. Written agreements are commonly used in professional and everyday life, but often take the form of a list of rules or details of a service offered. They are primarily used to protect the service provider from false expectations and claims against them. As such they rarely involve negotiation but simply state the obligations and limitations on all parties. Foster placements use such agreements. These are known as 'service agreements' or contracts. Obviously these will work best if administered in a user-friendly fashion.

We are concerned here, however, with different kinds of agreements – therapeutic or problem-solving agreements. These impose more stringent requirements if they are to have a chance of working. They are called 'contingency agreements', they have no legal implications but are personal documents used to solve disputes within families. They can contribute to changing behaviour patterns and are especially useful when involving teenagers. There are well-researched guidelines which if followed produce impressive results in overcoming disputes. You will see that all that has been said in this chapter is pertinent to producing effective agreements. In producing these attention should be paid to the following detail:

- Clarity of goals and tasks needs to be explicit.
- Negotiation and compromise to be patiently and thoroughly pursued.
- The action plan should be genuinely subscribed to by everybody involved.
- The advantages for all parties, including parents, care and professional workers (if they are involved), need to be stated. This is very important both to enhance motivation but also to ensure that genuine negotiation has taken place.
- There must be shared responsibility and fair penalties for all parties, including parents as well as the young person. This demonstrates to the young person that careful thought has gone into the process and that genuine commitment is involved.
- Effective monitoring and frequent reviews should be built in. This provides a framework for troubleshooting and some assurance that burdens will not be carried for too long. A week or fortnight at the outside is long enough for a contingency agreement to run. The object is not to create a regime of living by agreements but to restore a natural and more spontaneous ethos of problem-solving within a family and improve parent/teenager relationships.
- Where it is possible write the agreement down and get everybody to sign it. The young person can be very reassured by seeing that their parents take things seriously enough to commit themselves in this way. The adults avoid arguments if the young person can be referred to their own agreed statements of intent. It will only work if the negotiation is genuine and young people cannot excuse themselves by saying they had no option but were forced to comply. The process ensures that common mistakes which lead to conflict are avoided. An example of a written agreement where targets are clearly defined follows.

A Family Agreement

The object is to work towards fewer arguments and less tension within the family. To start the process the issue of coming in late will be addressed.

1   **Dilesh agrees to be home by 10.30pm** when there is school the following day. He will be given 2 tokens each night he achieves this. Also 5 extra bonus tokens for every three consecutive nights he achieves this. He can exchange these tokens according to the schedule previously arranged.
    ● *The advantages* to Dilesh are that he can work for things he has chosen and be in control of that. He will also know there will be no nagging or verbal disapproval.
    ● *The disadvantages* of failing to keep the agreement will be that he will have fewer tokens to exchange and could lose face and return to being nagged.

2   **Mum agrees to keep the token system up to date and to talk with Dilesh** about extra items he may wish to include on his menu of things to work for. She will not ask Dad to tell Dilesh off even if he comes in late.
    ● *The advantages* to her will be that her anxiety will be reduced, and pleasant rather than negative communications with Dad and Dilesh will increase.
    ● *The disadvantages* will be that if she fails to keep to her tasks the agreement will be null and void, and she will have to accept responsibility for renegotiating and for a return to increased levels of anxiety.

3   **Dad agrees to support Mum** and provide the outings and goodies promised to Dilesh when requisite tokens are earned, provided that he has been consulted about these.
    ● *The advantages* to him will be that he avoids being used to tell Dilesh off and does not have the upset of dealing with the anxiety his wife experiences, which in turn makes him angry. There should be increased peace and less arguing.
    ● *The disadvantages* if he fails to keep to the above are that the agreement will be null and void and he will have lost an opportunity to have less arguing and more peace. He will also have to renegotiate from a weaker position.

4   **There will be a meeting in a week's time on 8 October 1998 at 2.30pm to review the situation**. Revision of the detail in the agreement may be necessary, or, if progress indicates, the system could be finished. (An entirely new contract would be possible if it was ever needed again.)

Signed

Dilesh
Dad
Mum   Date

Finally, an agreement which looks like a list of rules and conditions laid upon the young person will not work or be useful.

Within the above example it would be possible to include a response cost element. This is dealt with in detail in Chapter 9, reference Session 5, though this would make quite a long agreement even longer.

It is worth repeating that it is important in the early stages to attend to detail and the process of negotiation. When this is done success is the most probable outcome.

6 The role of cognitive behavioural theory

Introduction

In the living with teenagers course parents frequently find a profound change takes place in the way they look at things. One Asian father reported, 'When I started the course I was hard-headed, but in the end the course has made me see things in a different light'. Parents are also often grappling with young people who are dealing with even more perplexing changes in the view they have of themselves and the world around them. Another parent reported, 'It also helps me to be more tolerant and patient'.

Although we do not teach cognitive theory as such in the groups, it has a number of useful applications. It can be helpful in making sense of some of the perplexing and powerful feelings and contradictory views which arise and chart the changes which occur. Parents may also find it a base from which to develop coping strategies in their family situations. The model focuses attention upon the link between feelings which upset us and the thoughts which fuel these upsets and prevent useful resolution of day-to-day problems.

Recognising negative thinking

An example might be simple anxiety about taking exams. If extreme this could lead to a mental block and result in his or her inability to answer exam questions. The student may just scribble for a while and then leave the exam room early. One can imagine the whole range of emotions and thoughts which are generated by such an act. The cognitive model offers a comparatively simple way of making sense of this. The underlying premise is that it is not just events but the way we personally appraise them which creates tension, and leads to a downward spiral of hurt and habit which gets in the way of the fulfillment of our plans.

A simple example of the model illustrates its application to the exam incident in the following grid:

Event	Thoughts (self-talk)	Feelings	Outcome
An examination	I do not know my work ... I always let myself down	Anxiety ... physical discomfort	Leaves exam room early

Leaving an exam in such a frame of mind could create problems both for the young person and the parents. A habit of thinking 'I will always let myself down' could fuel a self-fulfilling prophecy and downwards spiral. Cognitive behaviour work proposes that if this pattern of thinking can be identified, it might be possible to generate alternative ways of interpreting events which could lead to more desirable outcomes. The following grid illustrates this:

Event	Thoughts (self-talk)	Feelings	Outcome
An examination	I do not know my work ... I always let myself down	Anxiety ... physical discomfort	Leaves exam room early
	I can prepare carefully ... I can do really good work	A greater measure of confidence and calmness	Does easy questions first, leaves hard ones until later. Time flies, does a good paper.

There can be a good deal more involved than superficially identifying alternatives as shown above. However, making the link between 'self-talk' and unhelpful feelings is the starting point.

Applications abound. Parents are often understandably anxious or enraged by teenagers' behaviour and attitude. (The way in which cognitive models explain and offer coping strategies to deal with anger and persistent anxiety are explored in greater detail later in this book.) Young people are in the process of discovering their own identity and often test out and embrace ideas which seem to contradict what they have accepted from their parents up until that point. Careful attention to what they are saying, or thinking, can help us see the sense they make of what is going on for them. Even though we may disagree with such a view, it can be crucial to gain feeling for and some empathy with it.

Tuning in to consistent thought patterns can offer clues that things are going wrong. We know, for example, that drug users often think and feel very left out of things, have a very poor opinion of themselves and seek companionship in undemanding peer groups. Eating disorders can have a similar backdrop of low self-esteem. (Such situations would need referring on to involve expert help and would be beyond the scope of the seven-week course outlined here.) Within the seven weeks of the course it is possible to begin a process leading to greater understanding and improved communication within a family. This can both prevent extreme situations developing and form a solid base from which to resolve more entrenched difficulties.

Collaborative style is essential

Even though it is easy to see and hear other people running themselves down and to see alternative, more positive ways of looking at things, it is not always helpful to give direct advice. If somebody thinks and believes they are useless or unworthy, other people's opinions will not make much impact. Their thoughts are their truth. They probably do not even realise that what they say, in their head, about themselves is so pervasive and influential. For this reason the first task is to find ways of helping them draw their own conclusions and see the link between their thoughts and bad feelings and ineffective action. Using the negative feelings grid already illustrated, or a similar written device, could help this process. A diary which identifies stressful situations and accompanying thoughts and feelings may be a good starting point.

We are not encouraging people to attempt a regime to solve all discomfort by some ill-advised random positive thinking. Obviously if a young person stays out all night every night it would be natural to be concerned and worried. If someone who is significant to a young person dies or is badly hurt it would be natural for them to be sad and behave untypically for some time. It is only when anxiety or depression or anger become pervasive and long-lasting that use of these methods in an intensive way is justifiable.

The principles can be used nonetheless in a preventative way. Using the grid or diaries starts a process of seeing the difference between thoughts and feelings. This is not always very easy to do.

A guide to unhelpful thoughts is that they are framed in inaccurate or unhelpful ways, which are *not true* as they stand, because they can cause one or more of the following scenarios:

- They *generalise*. For example, one young man believed he was 'unattractive and unlovable'. That was tantamount to him saying 'in every respect those descriptions fit me'. He was very withdrawn and inclined to be lazy about hygiene. However, he had a very bright mind and an attractive mop of hair and fetching smile when something pleased him. His unhelpful self-talk ruled out even his consideration of those good points.

- They *exaggerate*. Many parents believe their teenagers are 'out to hurt us'. This can extend to suspicion, so that even pleasant behaviour and gestures have a false motive. The 'out to hurt us', as it stands, says that everything they do has hurtful intent. It leaves no room to see the conciliatory and loving actions amongst the wind-ups. It is easy to see how this way of thinking could breed resentment and depression.

- They *make extreme evaluations* and judgements. A student told me how unbearable it was not to have been awarded a first class honours degree. The fact that he achieved a lower second, even after a year disrupted by panic attacks, was not something he could class as success. Less than 100% performance spelled failure for him. It is understandable that such internal, impractical personal goals generate a proneness to fear and despair.

- They *infer* far more than the evidence demonstrates. It is not uncommon for young people to be very secretive and to distort the truth. Some say that 'if people really knew what I was like they could never love me'. One teenager would never say what she wanted because she believed her parents would be cross and get angry with her. In fact they would have loved to help. However, she believed they did not love her and could not understand her need for pocket money. From that viewpoint she drifted into lying and stealing to avoid their displeasure. Her inferences far exceeded reality and made trouble for the whole family.

- They force the *application of moral absolutes* such as 'I must'/'should'/ 'ought' to wide areas of lives. Many parents give themselves a really hard time believing they ought to be in control or managing very complex situations faultlessly. In a group of parents whose offspring were diagnosed as having ADHD (Attention Deficit with Hyperactivity Disorder), several were extremely critical (and there was evidence that many who should have known better reinforced that view) of themselves for feeling so helpless faced with that mysterious and draining condition. Some believed they 'should' never have time off for themselves because being a parent of such children meant they 'ought' to dedicate all their energies to the young person in question.

It does not take much imagination to see how becoming trapped into such ways of thinking bears the seeds of emotional distress and gets in the way of planning life to allow for creative recreation which each individual needs and deserves. To put it another way, recognising our own, or our teenagers', unhelpful 'self-talk' is a way of identifying triggers which can lead to difficulties, that can also, once recognised, show us when evasive action and coping strategies need to be deployed.

Working for change

The most effective way of changing is for individuals to form alternative ways of thinking for themselves. 'Socratic dialogue' is the preferred method spoken of in the text books. This simply means asking open-ended questions, or using statements, reflecting back or prompts which encourage individuals to challenge their own established 'automatic thoughts'.

Logical or rational challenge

This comes from considering evidence which contradicts the target thought. It may involve analysing the shape of the thoughts, as we did above, and seeing if making the self-talk more precise begins to alleviate some of the pressure it creates. An example might be that the young man above, illustrating generalisation, considers whether his self-appraisal as being 'unattractive and unlovable' really does cover everything. He was teased at school for poor hygiene, but he also attracted a good deal of encouragement and praise for some of his academic work and ready wit. So he could be led and encouraged to embrace wider views – suggestions not directions being the clue.

An individual will only take up what suits them; they will just not see that the contradictions apply to themselves otherwise. No matter how much one girl's parents protested they loved her, she was fixed in her view that 'if people really knew what I was like they could never love me'. Until evidence which commended itself to her was apparent, change was unlikely.

Sometimes information from written texts or expert opinion persuade, sometimes it does not. So it is a shared search, a combined puzzle-solving exercise to arrive at individually effective challenges.

Practical tasks

These can be used to provide good evidence. One parent believed her son, who had considerable learning difficulties, could neither be taught to speak, except to swear, or to go out without creating mayhem. After work in a group she decided to attempt a carefully planned bus trip. She had things for him to do, and deliberately gave him as much attention as possible. To her surprise the trip worked well. From a cognitive point of view the results were startling. She had been feeling very depressed and helpless, feelings underpinned by thoughts that 'I cannot expect J to learn anything' and 'I am not capable of teaching him'. Her planned trip, which involved considerable risk of it not working, had dispelled those thoughts with undeniable practical evidence that they were not true in every circumstance. Her shift to such a buoyant mood was a delight for everyone involved.

Arousal control

Panic or acute anxiety can make planned rational action impossible. Whatever our intentions, if we have been frightened by, say, an offspring staying out all night, it is likely that we shall greet their homecoming with an anxious third degree inquisition or an angry demand for explanations to relieve our own distress. So calming strategies may play an essential part. Practising relaxation techniques may be useful. Deep breathing, muscle relaxation or meditation, perhaps with music in the background, and imaging could all help alleviate morbid rumination. (Imaging is a way of moving away from thinking which can be self-critical to a more creative activity [Silverstone, 1996].)

Another set of techniques are 'thought stoppers'; that is finding something which will interrupt the anxiety when we feel the early signs of it taking over – perhaps a rubber band on the wrist twanged to hurt and just cause us to catch a breath, or counting to ten, or punching our own hand. These are best used in conjunction with some positive affirmation or rational challenges, rehearsed or written on a small card, to be read before the heat of the moment overtakes us again.

Keeping track of progress

These methods involve far more than just talking about problems. They include a great deal of practise of practical tasks as plans are tested for their efficacy in each individual case. The tasks often include using some kind of measures or indicators to establish which way things are moving – for better or worse!

Anxiety levels rating: 1–100		Situation: going out with partner believing he saw all other women as more attractive than herself		
Week	Before outing	During outing	alternative thinking practised	After outing
1	91%	85%	Yes	50%
2	77%	60%	No	55%
3	80%	65%	Yes	30%
4	50%	35%	Yes	20%

Based on fact, the above example represents the first few weeks of an intervention. The target belief that needed challenging was that she was not an attractive or lovable person. She therefore interpreted every glance or comment her partner made to other women as evidence that she was unattractive. The challenges in effect affirmed evidence of her own worth and attractiveness.

Often such records are very encouraging; as the work develops they demonstrate small improvements which are easily missed or lost to memory when a bad spell is worked through.

Applying the model to anxiety

Information is shared with the client which is intended to help normalise their experience. Anxiety can be explained as a natural response to threat or danger. As such it creates strong automatic changes in the body, releasing adrenaline into the blood stream to prepare for fight or flight. This interferes with normal activity. Action rather than considered thought is typical of this mode. It also heightens awareness of and the search for signs of danger. This is a natural response, essential for our survival, but at times extreme levels of this very uncomfortable experience pervade into areas where no obvious danger exists, for example, during exams or public speaking. Along with that exaggerated sense of anxiety comes a desire to avoid the discomfort; hence reluctance to go out, or even think about the issues, or the desire to take refuge in the relief that alcohol or tranquillizers, or constant sympathetic company can provide. Those evasions serve only, in the long

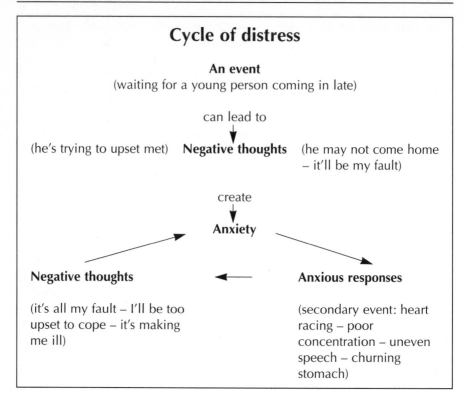

Cycle of distress

An event
(waiting for a young person coming in late)

can lead to

(he's trying to upset me!)   **Negative thoughts**   (he may not come home
– it'll be my fault)

create

Anxiety

Negative thoughts   **Anxious responses**

(it's all my fault – I'll be too   (secondary event: heart
upset to cope – it's making   racing – poor
me ill)   concentration – uneven
                                       speech – churning
                                       stomach)

run, to make matters worse. Anxiety can be represented diagrammatically in the following manner:
A cycle of distress is set in motion, making it very difficult for the sufferer to stay with the actual facts and circumstances which have triggered their discomfort. They will become so aroused that they retreat into their own hurt, or avoid it by going off at a tangent. When the young person comes in it is quite likely that they will be met with angry recriminations, or a hurt parent who cannot attend to the young person at all. Techniques suggested to overcome this unhelpful cycle are:

- Teaching about the nature of anxiety
- Distraction techniques
- The use of daily records of dysfunctional thinking
- And specific questioning to anchor the events feared in a real context.

Applying the model to anger

A good starting point is to realise that anger is an important human emotion which has useful as well as damaging functions. Also, it is not basically an uncontrollable impulsive reaction to events.

On the plus side anger is a positive emotion when it

- Tells us something threatening is happening
- Provides energy, the get up and go, to help us do something about it
- Communicates negative sentiments in an unmistakeable way.

On the down side anger is a destructive emotion because it

- Can prevent us from thinking constructively at looking at events dispassionately
- Makes it more likely that we will resort to aggressive tactics.

Current understandings and attempts to work with anger have leant heavily upon the work of Novaco (1985) and Meachenbaum (1985) in managing stress techniques. Both writers demonstrate the complexity of working with anger and the need to approach it from several fronts simultaneously. It is difficult to produce a diagram which captures the complexities but this may help:

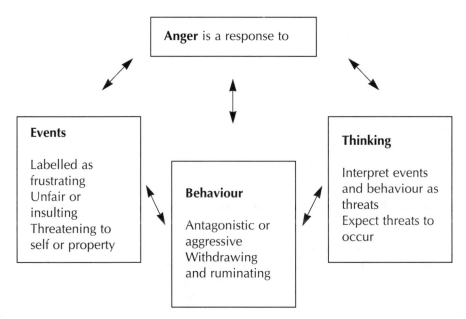

Anger can also provoke events, encourage behaviour and reinforce thinking which perpetuates the angry situation.

How to manage or cope with anger

Recognising triggers

First, attempt to recognise triggers. These will be very specific to any individual – found in a young person who is seen as defiant or provocative or a situation where a request from a parent feels to be invasive and demeaning. The intention of the action is irrelevant; it is the meaning which is put upon it which creates the arousal and irritation. It will then be useful to devise ways to defuse the anger, perhaps by walking away or counting to ten; alongside that perhaps rehearse statements which offer alternatives to the habitual ones. 'I will not be provoked this time' might be a way of bringing the arousal under control by changing the thinking behind it. As well as this, think of ways of expressing the anger in constructive ways: 'I am really p ... d off with constant arguing ... and will listen to you if you will listen to me'. In other words, begin to practice communication skills.

Understanding how anger works

Second, understand how anger works and how to communicate, to make it work for you. Learn to be assertive rather than aggressive, and use 'I' statements rather than 'you' statements. Listen to what the other person has to say, and try to understand, even if you do not agree with their point of view.

Practice alternative strategies

Third, practice, practice, practice alternative strategies and think about anger and the most helpful way to manage or use it to genuine advantage. Expect some set backs, but encourage persistence with the home tasks and with keeping diaries to monitor progress.

The groupwork programme

We include some of the features mentioned above in the programme; see Chapter 10 for the simplified way we present and use these ideas. Communication skills, such as listening and giving pleasant or conversely difficult messages in effective ways, are all practised if that is what group members select to do and need. They may not, however, be explicitly linked with identified anger or anxiety problems.

This chapter is written to encourage you to consider the part cognition plays, at a deep level, in the emotionally laden conflicts which arise in families. It would be essential to use the literature referred to for fuller understanding of cognitive theory and its applications if you were to attempt individual in-depth interventions. Our belief is that it is important, even in running a short programme, to be aware of issues which may arise and of the resources available to tackle them.

7 Groupwork skills: giving structure to groups for parents

Introduction

Running living with teenagers groups involves a combination of three essential skills:

- A sound grasp of social learning theory, the core of which is described in Chapter 4 of this book.
- Good planning to ensure that you attract a sufficiently large group of parents. A checklist for this is set out in Chapter 2.
- A sense of how to structure the sessions of the groupwork programme so that they have a constructive purpose with clear goals, while being flexible enough to deal with the worries and anxieties of each parent. The extent of these worries can be illustrated by some of the things they have said to us, such as, 'I feel like I am being punished for something I have done'. 'Who can help?' 'I am feeling a failure'. 'Where did I go wrong?' 'Why me?' 'I hate/have no love for my sons'.

It is the skill of being able to offer a clear structure, while at the same time paying enough attention to individual parents' needs, that will be addressed in this chapter. The emphasis will be on the *means* of doing this, rather than on the actual content of each of the sessions. The outline and content of each session of the living with teenagers programme is comprehensively outlined in Part Three of this book.

Tasks and role of the group leader

In training sessions we have had on setting up and running groups for parents of teenagers we have focused on the following as essential elements of the group leader's role:

- To create an informal, non-threatening working atmosphere. This can be encouraged in the first session by providing tea, coffee, biscuits or a glass of wine and a friendly atmosphere in which getting to know each other is a high priority. This probably seems like an obvious point but it is very evident that parents do feel very threatened by attending a group. This is clear from the feelings that parents have described to us in later sessions. A summary of these feelings is provided at the end of this chapter under the heading of 'Parents' feelings when they first attend a group'. Studying these comments should help group leaders to plan methods of making parents feel at ease. Some ideas are also given in our booklet 'Games and exercises used in fun and families groups' and in Part Three of this book.
- It is evident that people of different races, cultures and religions or disabled people will respond positively or negatively to different approaches. A good discussion of these issues is set out in Davis and Proctor (1989).
- Set goals for each session. Our experience suggests that you should not be over-optimistic about what you can get through in a two-hour session.
- Ensure everyone has a say and is involved – this requires helping to prevent people from dominating or diverting from the goals of the session. The object of the group is to allow parents to achieve an understanding of children's/young people's behaviours while allowing them the opportunity to select and practice the methods they want to use to influence those behaviours. Again, because of the diversity of approaches that are acceptable to people of different races, cultures or religions, it is important to avoid a 'Eurocentric' approach, that is a tendency to ignore or devalue any aspect of social, cultural or religious behaviour that is not basically white, European and Christian.
- It is important at the start for group leaders to set the ground rules by stating their commitment to anti-discriminatory practice. This then allows group leaders to challenge sexist or racist remarks if they arise during group sessions. A way of doing this which involves parents is to develop a Group Charter. Ideas for this are set out in Part III, Chapter 8, in Session 1.

- Give positive encouragement to everyone's efforts; be clearly encouraging and don't ignore or talk over people's responses. In particular, avoid any response that might be viewed as negative or threatening to parents. The building up of informal support and confidence among group members is a vital task for group leaders.
- Regularly refer people to the underlying theoretical principles. This can be done through the use of small group exercises and games. Parents find it easier to apply the theoretical examples when they are applied to individual circumstances. The use of exercises also helps to identify individuals who are lost or confused.
- Use your knowledge of group members to know when to help, for example, with difficulties with literacy. (This information will be available to you from your pre-group home visits.) Also, invite people to share their positive experiences with the group.
- Use a range of interesting material: video, articles, case examples, role play. Good material encourages participation, it should have practical relevance to parents and should ideally assist parents to practice parenting skills. Good material should also be non-sexist and non-racist. Poor material is usually too theoretical, has little practical relevance and, if done individually (rather than in pairs or small groups), fails to encourage group cohesion.
- Home tasks need to be negotiated at the end of each session and time given at the start of each subsequent session for feedback. This allows and encourages mutual support, problem-solving and the growth of confidence. A good example of this happening was when a parent insisted, in discussion with the group leaders, that her teenage sons would not comply with any request made of them. When she was able to discuss this in a small group with other parents she was able to identify that she always made her requests by shouting at them. Other parents suggested to her to try making requests in a calm and quiet voice. In the feedback the following week she was delighted to inform the group that this strategy had been very successful! Her delight and dramatic growth in confidence was an inspiration to the rest of the group.
- Always evaluate each session and each group to find out what went right or wrong.
- Have fun!

We have found from experience that achieving all these objectives is an impossible task for one group leader, and we would strongly recommend the use of two group leaders, both of whom have been involved in the planning of the group and feel comfortable working together. We have indicated in Chapter Two on planning that it is helpful to have female and male co-leaders, and also black workers where groups are being run for, or when they include, black families.

Basic procedures for discussion groups

Martin Herbert (1988) describes a set of procedures for running parent groups adapted from the work of D. and F. Johnson. I have adapted these procedures to make them specifically relevant to living with teenagers groups:

- *Define terms and concepts*   Groups require a shared language to hold a purposeful discussion. Words like 'discipline', 'punishment', 'problem behaviour' all have specific meanings within social learning theory as opposed to their everyday use. It is helpful, therefore, to find agreement and to give examples, where possible, to illustrate a word or a concept's meaning.
- *Negotiate and/or establish goals*   Clarify the goals or objectives of every session (see Part III for the content of each session). Allow time for 'homework' tasks to be discussed and, where possible, relate these to the learning tasks for each session.
- *Encourage free and fair discussion*   Encourage individuals in the free (but fair) expression of ideas, feelings, attitudes, openness, reactions, information and analysis. Do not allow the 'scapegoating' or bullying of any one member. Ground rules about confidentiality, racism, sexism and the importance of everyone having a say should be agreed at the group's outset.
- *Integrate the material*   Continually refer back to the learning that has been achieved over succeeding group sessions. The groupwork sessions are designed to gradually build up the parent's understanding of teenagers and their confidence in their parenting skills.
- *Encourage the application of the discussion material*   Ask group members to identify the relevance of the learning material to their own lives. Encourage them to apply the positive things and report back to the group the 'feedback' they received from their efforts.

Effective group intervention

According to Martin Herbert (1988), a group intervention will be effective if the following criteria are met:

- The group *climate* should be warm, accepting and non-threatening.
- Learning should be seen as a *co-operative* activity.
- *Learning* should be seen as the primary purpose of the group.
- Every member of the group should *participate*.
- Group sessions should be stimulating and *pleasurable*.
- *Evaluation* should be seen as a central part of the group's activities.
- Participants should come *regularly* and be prepared.

Troubleshooting – dealing with individual contributions

Even if all the points raised above have been attended to, there are some situations that arise that require confident but sensitive handling. The most common ones include:

- People who go on at length, restricting the time left for others.
- People who drift off the main point to matters that are interesting but are outside the scope of the group.
- People who make racist or sexist remarks and practice other forms of negative discrimination.
- People who can dominate the rest of the group.
- People who start up private, secondary conversations during group discussions.
- People who make no (or very minimal) contribution to the group.

If these problems occur it is worth considering the points set out in the paragraph on effective group intervention above. For example, if the group climate has for some reason become 'threatening' or creates anxiety for parents, it would be a reasonable response for parents to feel unwilling to contribute. A useful thought as far as troubleshooting is concerned is to work on the assumption that 'the best solutions are those you find before you have got the problem'. In other words, good planning and attention to the procedures referred to in the paragraphs above *should* help you to avoid having to become involved in anything more than minor troubleshooting!

The co-leader has an important role in watching for these problems and intervening where they think necessary, and also in supporting the other group leader's attempts to do so. The leaders should also consider strategies to cope with these difficulties in their planning meetings between each group session. The importance of ensuring every one has a say is a vital role for the group leaders and should be stressed at the outset of each session when feedback on the weekly task is sought.

Where group leaders need to intervene to curtail someone's contribution, this needs to be done sensitively without causing offence. This requires the use of a range of skills which most of us practice everyday without thinking about them:

- Initially, it is important to get eye contact with the person speaking.
- If this can't be done simply by looking at them, try a more active method such as standing up, moving to the flip chart or video, dropping a book or a pen, etc. to attract their attention.
- Once you have their attention, always give a positive reason for interrupting them (e.g. need to let everyone have a say, or need to move on to the next session) and thank them (where relevant) for their contribution.
- If people have individual matters they wish to raise that are not relevant to the group task, offer to see them at the end of the session so that the group as a whole can proceed.

If one individual creates persistent difficulties it may be worth thinking about where the leader and co-leader sit – for example, sitting between two parents who keep having secondary conversations during group sessions. Alternatively, the co-leader can sit next to a person who has been identified as needing encouragement, or discouragement!

If one individual has a persistent pattern of behaviour that continues to effect the group it is preferable to see them on their own to discuss this. Our experience has been that if such problems are not tackled by the group leaders, the group participants will deal with it, and often in a less sensitive and more critical manner.

A good example of this relates to dealing with situations where parents may make a racist, sexist or other form of discriminatory comment. It has been said earlier, in the section on the role of group leader, that dealing with such comments is much easier if, in the first session, the group leaders have set out their intention to respect people of any race, religion, culture, gender, disability and sexual orientation. Assuming such a comment is made, the following steps have been found to be helpful.

First, it is helpful to be clear in your own mind that the comment is racist, sexist or discriminatory in some way and why. If you are not sure, it is helpful to ask the person who made the comment to clarify what they were saying. For example, a white parent in a living with teenagers group in Leicester was concerned about her 16-year-old son obtaining drugs from school and referred to the drug dealers as being African-Caribbean. The group leader was not sure, at the time the comment was made, whether she was being implicitly racist by assuming the dealers were African-Caribbean (sterotyping), or just making a factual statement that didn't rely upon hearsay. The group leader dealt with it by saying 'I am sorry, I am not sure whether I understand the meaning of what you are saying. Were you suggesting that all drug dealers are African-Caribbean or that your son was approached by a drug dealer who happened to be African-Caribbean?' The parent clarified that the latter was the case. The group leader was then able to proceed, while being able to remind the group of the need to respect people of all races, as agreed in the 'ground rules' (referred to in the Group Charter in Part III, Chapter 8, Session 1).

Second, if the statement needs no clarification because it is obviously racist, sexist, etc., from the outset, or if, after clarification, it does seem offensive, then it is vital to draw the attention of the group to it and to refer the group back to the Charter discussed and agreed in Session 1 of the group. This can then give the parent responsible the opportunity to apologise and the group the opportunity to learn from the experience. For example, a parent was using a token system and had added their own variation of giving their teenager black tokens to note bad behaviour. The parent immediately recognised, when it was drawn to his attention, that this was conveying a negative image of black people by modelling for his son a connection between 'badness' and 'blackness'. The parent apologised and the group learned from the experience.

It is important to say at this point that most parents who attend groups will probably not have had the opportunity to attend racism awareness or anti-racism courses. Consequently, their level of awareness of the impact of discrimination will be less than that of professional staff, which will inevitably limit what can be achieved in terms of learning. The result is that a balance needs to be struck between using opportunities that arise to assist parents to increase their awareness, while recognising that the primary purpose of the group is to improve teenage/parent relationships, not to offer an anti-discriminatory awareness course. Nothing in this paragraph, however, should imply that group leaders should condone discriminatory comments. In this respect we would take the view that 'If you are not part of the solution, you must be part of the problem' (Anderson, Osada and Thompson, 1994, p. 16).

Troubleshooting – strategies for groups

There are three types of common difficulties that can arise in living with teenagers groups:

Groups that are stuck

By 'stuck' we mean that the group, or a proportion of the group, finds some aspect of the theoretical material difficult to accept. For example, one group found it hard to accept that recording behaviour on the recording charts would have any beneficial effect. If groups become 'stuck' it is most likely to happen in Sessions 1–3 because, at this stage, there is a high level of belief that 'nothing will work'. In addition, any beneficial changes will not have started to show sustained success at this point.

The best approach in this situation is to press on with the programme, making sure that all the theoretical ideas have been rigorously covered. At the same time it is important to *acknowledge* the reservations expressed without becoming defensive.

In the example given above, of the group that doubted the effectiveness of recording, an insight by a parent at the start of Session 2 helped them to move on. The parent concerned chose the task of recording the squabbling and fighting between their teenage son and daughter. After she had recorded it for a week she recognised that the fights had reduced. She expressed the view to the other group members that the reduction had occurred because she had stopped getting involved in the fights, and because her response when they occurred was to record them rather than to get embroiled in them. Session 2 started, therefore, with a better appreciation of the value of the home tasks.

Groups that become negative or defensive

A negative group is one in which the group members predominantly report no progress. It can often be a feature of small groups of 4–6 people that one person, who is making no progress, is very dominant. Obviously some of the strategies referred to in the preceding section on troubleshooting are relevant here. In addition, as with 'stuck' groups, it also tends to be a feature of Sessions 1–3.

The best way to help such groups is based on the old adage 'nothing succeeds like success'. This strategy might involve the following actions. Choose a parent who has obviously had some success and then let them start the feedback session, thereby creating a positive mood. In addition, during the feedback encourage the parents who are experiencing less favourable results to speak about any small success or insight they have had and be very positive about this. It is also worth asking parents who are having some success to suggest ideas which might help those who are not.

If a parent is clearly in great difficulties it can pay dividends to offer some individual help between sessions in order to help them achieve some success, however limited. Just as with 'stuck' groups, it is unlikely that a group will be negative for all seven sessions, so pressing on with the programme while acknowledging the difficulties usually achieves the desired improvements in parent/teenager relationships.

Groups that lack cohesion, or have groups within the group

The wide mix of people who come to living with teenagers groups is usually a very positive feature and all seem to benefit from the diversity of backgrounds. However, on occasions, the group can fail to be mutually supportive or a small clique can develop within the group. Again a range of strategies need to be used:

- Make sure everyone has a say by encouraging quiet members and controlling dominant members.
- Deliberately design small group exercises to encourage parents to work together with *all* other parents in the group.
- Encourage whole group participation and discourage secondary conversations in the group.

A good outline of groupwork strategies and leadership roles is referred to in *A Handbook of Common Groupwork Problems* by Tom Douglas (Routledge, 1991).

Parents' feelings when first attending a group

The lists below are comments made by parents who attended two different fun and families groups in different geographical locations and at different times. The New Parks group was a fun and families group and the Hinckley group was a living with teenagers group. The most noticeable feature of the comments is the similarity between them, suggesting a very common set of experiences for parents who are experiencing behaviour difficulties with their children.

New Parks: Leicester 1997

I can't cope
I am the only one
My child's a little devil
I don't know where to turn
Who can help?
I am feeling a failure
Is it all my fault?
Where did I go wrong?
Why me?

Hinckley: February–April 1997

I'm the only one
Losing my grip
I hate/have no love for my child
Couldn't function as a parent
My child doesn't like me
Relief if my child is not there
Beating against a brick wall
Paranoid
Dread and fear of the future
Feel like drink, drugs or escape
Jealous of other parents
What am I doing wrong?
Other people think your children are good.

Part III

The seven-week living with teenagers programme

8   Understanding behaviour: Sessions 1 and 2

Format of the seven-week programme

The objective of this programme is to present ideas in a practical way so that they can be tested and practised in parents' own homes.

Before looking at the sessions in detail it is helpful to look briefly at the question of home visits. As a general rule we attempt to visit all would-be participants in their own home prior to the start of the group, unless there are obvious reasons for not doing so. There are a number of important tasks to achieve. Sharing factual information about the course and exploring the need to attend all the sessions is important. As each week develops in an incremental way, it is unhelpful to drop in and out of the process. Both the support available from other participants in the proposed group and the responsibility towards them is worth discussing. Make the point that it is not just a talking course but that practical tasks are also central to the process.

During home visits it is sometimes possible to get a better feel of existing interactions between family members, and also information about particular needs can be discreetly explored and taken account of. Examples might include the need for interpreters, or special preparation to allow people who cannot read to be supported and not exposed in the group.

Emphasis on reassurance and encouragement generates enthusiasm. Sometimes, however, parents decide it is not for them and it is far better for everybody that this is worked out before the group than part way into it. Absentee and resistant members can profoundly effect a group process. Normally we try to take up slack for one missed meeting by a home visit when the reason for staying away is genuine. We find that it is virtually impossible to do this for more than one session without the group suffering.

A this point we share with parents our philosophy that they know their own teenager best and are probably more expert than us on that subject. What the group provides is an opportunity to share and learn they are not alone. It also provides a systematic way of looking at difficulties and generating solutions to them. Quotations from parents who have done the course may be more eloquent than our own words to emphasise the effectiveness of joining the course.

During the home visit, it may be that questionnaires can be filled in if the parents seem keen to attend. This is part of our evaluation process (see, for example, the Teenage Behaviour and Communication Rating Scale, Appendix A). Our practice is to ask that the same form be filled in again at the end of the course so that comparisons can be made. We are still developing questionnaires to serve our own purpose, which is essentially practical feedback. They may not meet the strictest academic requirements for validity and reliability but have the advantages of being simple to complete, and the positive results are appreciated by parents.

This section of the book is meant to provide a detailed guide to running a group. The information cannot include everything, though it probably contains far more than can be fitted into the time available. So use the outline flexibly and adapt it to your own needs. We know from our own and others' experience that the framework produces good results. Experience has taught us that it is more important to be with the parents and go at their pace than try to cram in too much information. It cannot be stressed too strongly that this is a sharing, rather than a teaching, exercise.

Each session is divided into roughly two parts. The first part is used to present and explore the group's reaction to the idea of the week. In the second part the group subdivides so that each individual can select and, with the help of a smaller, more intimate group, share the task they will undertake at home. This also enables the group leaders to provide more individual attention when that is necessary.

This part of the book is organised with two intentions. Each session will be presented in outline. This should provide a check list for those who are experienced in theory and groupwork. Obviously you can amend it to suit your own style and situation. It is useful, however, to have some idea, in this kind of programme, of how much material to include, and the time required to present that effectively without either rushing things or seeming to be too slow. It could be useful to have a copy of this to hand when you are leading a group. A warning would be not to adhere slavishly to the 'programme', but to use it as a prompt. You will then feel more relaxed and be able to create a warm and flexible atmosphere.

The checklist will be followed by an expanded presentation of the material included, and comments from our experience about how things have developed in our groups. This is intended for those who are newer to the work – hopefully it will provide both practical information, and also something of the feel of what happens in groups using this programme.

Session 1: being clear and defining behaviour carefully

1 Personal introductions

- Warm-up game: throw the ball to name of person that you can remember.
- Aims of the group: put key aims of group on flip chart and ask participants to add any other matters they wish. Include anti-discriminatory practice.

2 Main theme: learning to be clear

- Describe difficult behaviours and list parents' descriptions on flip chart.
- Use Dave Allen video to look at ways parents describe behaviour.
- Introduce Woolly Exercise.
- Look at the characteristics of a good, clear description of behaviour.
- Finding a place to start: looking at chains of behaviour with 'Absolutely Fabulous' video.

3 Coffee break

4 Defining behaviour

- Defining behaviour exercise: group leaders divide group into two small groups and the task is for each parent to select and define carefully one behaviour they want to work on. This is done with the assistance of other parents and group leaders.

5 Home task

- Describe use of recording charts and the value of 'tracking' behaviour.
- Consider other ways of recording: audio, video, notebooks or diaries.
- Give out recording charts and folders for parents.
- Offer phone numbers for those who may need back-up.

Session 1: being clear, defining and recording behaviours

There are some important preliminaries, especially if the group do not all know each other. For example, we have tried a range of warm-up games. Generally those that do not rely on the written word are best. One that we have found consistently good is to ask all the participants to introduce themselves. Then ask the participants to throw a soft ball to someone whose name they can remember. This continues until every person has received the ball at least once. This game can be even more fun if a toy ball such as a 'Bumble Ball' is used. A 'Bumble Ball' is a battery operated soft plastic ball that shakes violently and is difficult to throw in a straight line. However, feedback from groups has shown us that making introduction too long or elaborate is unhelpful as parents are often eager to get on to the work of the sessions.

Nonetheless, some of the following items in the introductions list (under the heading 'Aims of the group') are important to present in an informal but fairly brisk and businesslike fashion. The important thing is to make the participants feel comfortable and hopeful. It helps to have an idea about the overall shape of the course and particularly of the session. The parents need to know also that they have some say in adjusting the format if they wish. A group charter or ground rules list may go some way to reassuring them.

The group needs to know who you are, your philosophy and interests, perhaps your skills and the way you prefer to work. They also need to develop trust in each other as well as to believe that you are interested in what they are doing. That may sound trite, but if a leader is too preoccupied with what they are presenting it can erode such confidence. It is more important to attend to, and be thoroughly familiar with, the group members and their agendas than it is to have ready-made answers and ideas for them.

Make sure they have material and understand how it is best used. Handouts can be counter-productive if they are fumbled through and take attention away from what is happening in the group.

Aims of the group

Within the preliminaries it is useful to set out the aims of the group and some of the philosophy behind the programme, along the lines of the topics summarised here:

1 *Understanding behaviour* The theory behind the group may not be of huge interest to parents, but what they will be keen to know is that the course attempts to show how behaviour is influenced and established.

For this reason, understanding the principles which control behaviour, if these can be explained in plain language, will capture their interest. At its simplest all that needs to be said is that, generally speaking, behaviour is taught. We can therefore teach alternative behaviours if we are dissatisfied with the way our younger children currently behave. It is also possible to discourage unwanted behaviours, or help them to be 'unlearned'.

2 *Practical alternatives*   Above all, the course is about trying out and testing alternative strategies of influencing behaviour. It is not the discussion that is primarily important, but rather the home tasks, and the experience gained in comparing what everyone has discovered there.

3 *Positive effectiveness and fun*   Our emphasis is always on the positive alternatives. We work hard to generate ways of being with our children which are varied, interesting and fun. This is because we know this works best.

4 *Parents are the real experts about their own children*   This is because they spend most time with them, and are closest to them emotionally. They will find which strategies work best, because only they know how their own families operate. All we hope to do through the group is to offer a greater number of ideas, and the means of selecting the best ones to suit each parent.

5 *Confidential – Informal – Sharing (CIS)*   In the group we can all learn a lot, and everyone will best contribute to that process if the CIS theme is pursued. We must try to develop trust, friendliness and a genuine sharing, and even the leaders' personal experiences should be included in that.

6 *Commitment*   To the full seven sessions, to doing the home tasks and feeding back honestly is important.

7 *Ground rules*   There will be some things the leaders wish to introduce, but participants may also have items about which they need reassurance.

Presenting and establishing ground rules

Presenting ground rules is very important but requires sensitivity. In some groups people are very keen to set ground rules; in others they do not really see the need for it. Establishing ground rules can create quite an inhibiting and formal atmosphere if it is not handled well. It may be better to leave it until the second session when people are more comfortable with each other.

Below is one format we have tried.

Group Charter

In any group it helps the smooth running of meetings if everyone can say what their special needs or expectations are. This handout provides space to list your preferences about some ground rules for the group. Once they are agreed, they can be written down and kept for reference. Additions or changes can be made whenever people feel the need for alteration or clarification. It is most important that everyone feels comfortable and safe to say what they want without fear or favour. We have an anti-discriminatory practice policy, and although the first eight lines are left for group members to fill in, we have filled in the last two lines because these items are important to the Centre.

1 . . . .
2 . . . .
3 . . . .
4 . . . .
5 . . . .
6 . . . .
7 . . . .
8 . . . .
9 We should try to avoid language which causes offence or show disrespect to another individual's views or customs, whatever their race, creed, gender or sexual orientation.
10 Any personal information shared in these sessions must be treated as strictly **confidential** and not repeated outside of the group sessions.

One way we have found of approaching this is to write the aims of the group (p. 96) on a flip chart in the form of headings, and then leave a blank space at the end for group members to add their preferences about the group. This can then be displayed each week so that anyone can add to it at any time, ensuring that group members can contribute to the list when they feel comfortable and confident to do so, rather than feeling pressured to do so in the first session.

Learning to be clear

The main theme of the first session, after dealing with the 'getting to know you', is helping people to stand back from their situation and learn to describe more clearly the teenage behaviours which irritate, trouble or drive parents to distraction. One way to start is to ask them to offer one or two descriptions to put on the flip chart. You will get some interesting colloquial descriptions like 'pigs would be embarrassed to live in his bedroom' or 'she just won't listen to a word I say'. Do not comment at this stage because the purpose is to get some fairly general descriptions like 'tantrums' and 'defiance' so that the discussion can be developed. There will probably also be some heavily value-laden and judgemental terms used, such as she is 'jealous', he is 'aggressive' and so on. Leave these to one side and introduce the 'Woolly' exercise as a handout.

Handout: 'Woolly' exercise

Tick the boxes according to whether you think the description in column one is clear and precise, or, on the other hand, 'woolly' and unclear and might lead to confusion or misunderstanding.

Description	Tick if 'Clear'	Tick if 'Woolly'
1 Dinesh is always on the go!		
2 Sally slams the door when she passes through it.		
3 Reena pays attention to requests.		
4 David carries on playing pool after his time.		
5 Anita shows evidence of hyperkinetic syndrome.		
6 Paddy picks his nose.		

The 'Woolly' exercise requires individuals to tick columns quickly to indicate whether they believe the descriptions offered are clear or woolly. There is no right or wrong answer – the beauty of this game is that we have never found a group where parents were unanimous in their conclusions. A discussion readily grows, or can be prompted when the results are collated. We then ask people to put up their hands if they believe each description is clear or woolly and collate the numbers on the flip chart. So in a group of ten people the chart may look like this:

Description	Clear	Woolly
1 On the go!	8	2
2 Slams the door	6	4
3 Attention to requests	1	9
4 Playing pool	5	5
5 Hyperkinetic	2	8
6 Picks his nose	9	1

The discussion can be developed by asking those who are unclear to put questions to those who were clear about a description which would help clear up their uncertainties. It seems to be particularly important to start by asking those who are unclear to seek more information. If you start with those who are clear, the exercise can become quite muddled and unhelpful. Discussions also flow more readily if you focus on those descriptions which found opinions evenly divided. In the figure above this would be descriptions two and four.

Defining behaviour

This discussion can be followed by the defining behaviour handout to be used in small groups. With this, participants start to practice being more precise. It may seem laborious but it is important to develop this skill of defining. Often people will believe they understand, but when they come to apply it still find themselves struggling. So it is very worthwhile to devise a number of practical tasks to test the progress, such as referring back to the flip chart and asking if they would like to redefine some of the behaviours first described. It is impossible to stress this too much. Later, if a programme is not working well, it will often be found that it was based on a loose definition of the selected behaviour. A further point that logically follows is that the issue of *defining* a behaviour is tied up with the business of *selecting* a behaviour to work on.

Behaviours in a chain

When working with parents of teenagers it is worth noting that the *selection*

Handout: defining behaviour

The following three descriptions have elements which are rather vague and general. Try to select the words which specifically say *what* the teenagers actually do.

- Sarah is a real pain in the neck, she is so defiant. Every time she is asked to do something she screams, shouts and dashes out of the room banging the door. She is so moody!
- Mira is always demanding and rude. When I have visitors or am doing housework she continually interrupts by shouting, throwing things and being a nuisance!
- Amrat drives me up the wall. Every time I speak to him he just 'grunts'. But when he wants some pocket money, he can be as 'nice as pie' and talks to me respectfully.

---

of a starting point is often quite difficult to decide upon. It is helpful to choose behaviours that illustrate the following:

- They can be seen. One parent was afraid her daughter was becoming strange because of incessant noises coming from her room; progress started when she moved from that concern to describe what was actually happening in her presence.
- They are happening within the home and to some extent, therefore, the parents have power to influence events. It is not helpful to choose behaviours reported from school or within the community with peers.
- Behaviours that are variations on one theme are best not looked at separately. For instance, if a young person frequently says 'no' when asked to wash, or get up in the morning, or stop teasing his sister, it may be necessary to cluster all the 'saying "nos"' together at this first deciding stage.
- Behaviours which occur one after the other are best dealt with by choosing one of them nearest the beginning of the chain.

The following diagram can be used to help parents understand the notion of behaviours progressing in a chain, and act as an introduction to this theme in the handout chart later in the chapter:

One → Thing → Leads → To → Another

Behaviours often follow a set pattern, one thing leading predictably to another. If we can tease out the separate components they can be arranged in an ascending order of severity. This can be a very useful skill in terms of locating a starting point in solving unacceptable behaviour patterns.

For example, complaints about tantrums – each tantrum involves a range of different actions. One 14-year-old followed a pattern which progressed from 1) answering back, 2) getting upset, 3) being really 'nice' (bribery), 4) whingeing and moaning, 5) demanding, 6) shouting, 7) demanding attention, 8) swearing at siblings, 9) throwing things, 10) banging doors, 11) threatening suicide, 12) stamping on things, 13) 'demolishing' his bedroom, 14) hitting parent and finally, 15) to swearing at parent.

We all tend to notice the most extreme behaviours first, and perhaps pay no attention at all to the less provoking ones. The chart below attempts to show the different phases a tantrum may go through as it develops.

Handout: one thing leads to another

1	answer back	These behaviours have often been overlooked or tolerated.	
2	upset	However they can be managed by firmness, or diversion, or reason.	
3	attention	Thus they make a good starting point to solve the bigger problems. By reducing these, those behaviours higher up the pattern will automatically be reduced.	Phase 1
4	'nice'	Here there is a clash of interests, or ground rules. This can feel like a 'wind-up', and in older children it may well be. A sense of mutual antagonism rapidly develops and makes control impossible	
5	throwing		
6	shouting		Phase 2
7	crying		
8	hitting sibling	These behaviours have a life of their own. They can be very intense. They are often not open to reason at all. The behaviour takes the person over and causes them to be out of control.	
9	demolishing		Phase 3
10	hitting parent		

Quite often the selected behaviour at this stage will not be the one eventually worked with. The process may start with a behaviour such as smoking but end with trying to improve the quality of communication. This does not matter because, on the way, important factors are uncovered and better understood. Perhaps a greater appreciation of what lies behind someone's mood emerges. It may be that a parent appreciates to a greater extent the effect their own anger or anxiety has in maintaining or exacerbating a situation.

It is important to have a number of exercises or some way of promoting a thorough discussion of why the language we use can assist in problem-solving. It is also necessary to examine quite closely some of the traps which await us as we make our selection. For example, highly emotive language has its use for expressing feelings and the degree of frustration and hurt experienced, but rephrasing can reduce a problem to more manageable proportions. 'Promiscuous' is a word which always conjures up strong feelings of judgement, or fear for the youngster's safety. If you ask 'what does "promiscuous" look like?' it might softened to 'talks to girls/boys all the time'. This is a great simplification but the theme is an important one to develop.

Tracking behaviours

Once a behaviour has been selected and defined, ways of observing it more objectively are explored. The difference between the record-keeping which we discuss here and star charts needs clarification. In the first week we want to help the parents to stand back and observe, just to collect information and reflect on it. Some will be eager to change behaviours and perhaps have been advised by other professionals to use star charts for this reason and may be rather cynical about them. We encourage parents simply to practise observing what is happening quite closely and not to try solutions until Session 3.

The use of charts or diaries is known to be useful. The chart overleaf illustrates the way in which understanding about the behaviours is built up. Not everyone will take to this immediately, but invariably most members of the group make good use of the idea and others are swept along in their enthusiasm. After a few days a typical chart could look like this:

Behaviour record chart

Time	8–9	9–10	10–11	11–12	12–1	1–2	2–3	3–4
Mon			✔		✔✔✔		✔	
Tues	✔	✔	✔		✔✔	✔		✔
Wed			✔		✔✔			
Thur	✔	✔	✔✔		✔	✔	✔	✔
Fri		✔			✔✔✔		✔	

✔ = Refusal to respond, i.e., shouting and stamping after being asked to do something, then walking away without doing it

From this information patterns can be seen: 11 to 12 is always trouble free; outbursts occur all day on Thursday; 12 to 1 is a particularly bad time. Maybe you would select to examine 12 to 1 more thoroughly? That could reveal some important leads and make the task more manageable.

The information could be transposed to a progress graph. In the one below the number of refusals per day are simply added together. So the first Thursday shows up as peaking with most refusals. On the first Friday a response cost programme (see Chapter 10) is introduced to try to reduce the number of outbursts. It is quite usual for the behaviour to get worse at this stage for a while; it is important to warn parents that this may well happen because they will see this and give up at this point. In other words they were probably doing exactly the right thing but were not encouraged to see it through. It can be empowering to realise that, with a little fine tuning, their own plans are probably the best. Notice the downward trend from the second Thursday – it is important and offers encouragement. The setback on the third Wednesday is not unusual and is probably best ignored.

We always ask that good behaviours are included on the graph or chart. These have been omitted from the example opposite for simplicity's sake. They are not defined so closely, but it is useful to strike a balance. An example from an intervention conducted at home, and recorded over 30 days, illustrates the point.

In the intervention, the target behaviour, hitting, was recorded three times. Good behaviour was observed on 59 occasions. Arguments were recorded 37 times. This revealed that arguing was more of a problem than the hitting! Also that good behaviour outweighed both! The work refocused on the

Progress graph

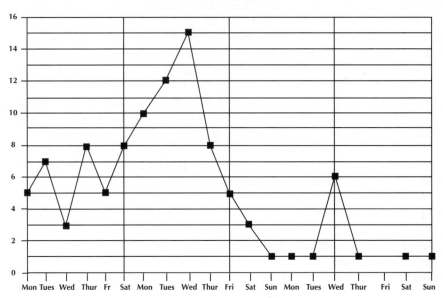

arguments, and increasing positive communication skills became the target. This recording is set out in the bar chart below.

Recording of good and bad behaviours

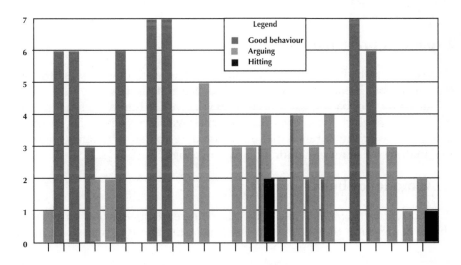

With teenagers it may be most appropriate to explain what you are doing, and perhaps invite them to keep their own records to see if parents and the young person agree on the approximate accuracy of each other's efforts. It depends on the behaviour and the young person and the objective of the parent; they alone will be able to judge which is best in their circumstances.

We have also found that making audio or video recordings – when practical and acceptable – can be a further way of recording. One sixteen-year-old was shocked to the core to hear himself in a full-blown temper. 'I sound like a three year old,' he observed, and the experience was more effective than endless complaining.

The home task for session one is to practise recording a behaviour each parent has selected. Observing events in this way can be most rewarding, but it is a real skill to be practised and learnt.

The final section of this session is crucial to the development of the whole course. It involves ensuring that each person goes home with a task they feel comfortable with, and the necessary forms to help them. Enough time should be left in order to allow each person to have an opportunity to make a real selection, and have discussed it with the others. Some will find the work easy, others will need a lot of help if they are to succeed. The most common mistake is to take on too much work, and select too difficult or vague a behaviour to record.

If, by the end of this session, you have enthused parents sufficiently to go home ready to attempt this first step of recording and observing, you will have done well.

Session 2: putting behaviour into context

Expanded presentation

This session is the key to the whole course. It may seem that there is little on the agenda but in fact there is much to practice and discuss.

During the feedback regarding the previous week's home tasks, a sense of the context in which the behaviour is set will have been realised. This session is devoted to trying to refine that understanding so that it becomes a useful tool in due course for generating plans for change.

ABC model of behaviour

A good warm-up game is as follows: in pairs, each speaks to their partner about something they are really enthusiastic about – either serious,

---

Session 2: putting behaviour into context

Introductions

1 • Welcome
  • Brief recap on last week
  • Feedback on home task

2 **Main theme: the ABC model of behaviour**

  • Warm-up 'ignoring' exercise, speaking in pairs
  • Input on the ABC sequence – triggers and pay-offs.

3 **Exercise 1** Handout on 'Dilesh': exercise and feedback (teenage ABC).

4 **Exercise 2** Extract from video, 'Teenagers, Living with the Enemy' (teenage ABC), or some other excerpt, e.g. 'Harry Enfield and Chums 1997'.

5 **Coffee break**

6 **Adolescent development**

  • 'What is normal behaviour?' discussion.
  • Developmental stages of adolescence.
  • Differing expectations according to race, gender, culture, religion, disability or sexual orientation.

7 **Home tasks**

  • Encourage parents to keep on recording tick charts and diaries, etc.
  • Also include building up ABC observation.

---

outrageous or funny. For the first 45 seconds the listener shows all the signs of being disinterested – yawning, turning away, etc. Then, for the next 45 seconds, the listener switches to listening attentively and showing it. Even though this is recognised as artificial it promotes good discussion.

The effect that the listener's demeanour has on the behaviour of speaking, both with regard to the speaker's feelings and to their ability to speak effectively, is most noticeable. Similarly, the after-effects on the speaker are also seen. Invite people to say how they felt being on the receiving end of being ignored compared with being listened to. Draw out the way the behaviour of speaking was influenced, made difficult by ignoring, but encouraged and made easier by attention. Then, enquire how it felt to do the ignoring and attending, and the difference between them. This exercise helps parents to recognise that the behaviour (talking) was influenced by the trigger (group leader's request to the parents to talk to each other) and the pay-off (either being listened to attentively or ignored). It is usually guaranteed to produce plenty of fun and laughter!

The session then moves on to looking at the concept of putting behaviour in its context. This is most important in helping parents to obtain an understanding about why particular behaviours might occur and the meaning they might have for their teenager. The model we use to help parents make this discovery is the ABC model. Listed below is the meaning of each letter:

- **A = Antecedents,** that is, events which come before the behaviour. In younger children we look particularly for what comes *immediately* before – usually seconds rather than minutes. However, in considering teenager behaviour, the influence of more distant triggers may be important. This is referred to in the paragraph below.
- **B = Behaviour** which we have selected to observe or change.
- **C = Consequences,** that which comes immediately after the behaviour. Again, with teenagers, more distant pay-offs may be important.

A great deal of research has gone into this simple ABC model; so we know that the triggers and the pay-offs can determine how well a behaviour is established and maintained.

Behaviours are a response to signals, cues or stimuli. So in looking for the 'As' or triggers we are normally looking for:

1 *Setting events* – provide opportunity for behaviours to be tried out and practised. Usually some specific time (getting ready for school, bedtime or meal time), or a particular place (clothes shops) or a person (best friend, girl/boyfriend) can be identified and associated with troublesome behaviour. Behaviour is more often than not a response to one or more of these features. So, if a pattern of behaviour or habits have been formed, changing the 'As' can bring about dramatic changes quite quickly.

2 *Prompts* – for a behaviour. For example a 'don't do that' could well prompt and encourage a teenager to do something which they may not otherwise have even thought about. Alternatively, requests made in an

angry or grumpy fashion, such as 'go and clear up that pigsty you call a bedroom' will predictably lead to unhelpful or difficult behaviour.

3 *Examples to copy* – copycatting or, more technically, modelling, simply describes the way teenagers love to mimic and imitate what they see and hear. If they see something on television or video they will want to try to do the same! If they hear swearing they may copy that too! If we want a behaviour to occur the best starting point is to show the teenager what we do want; this is often much more powerful than just telling them.

Once a behaviour is performed the effect of the consequences – 'Cs' – or pay-offs also have an important part to play. If a behaviour is met with pleasant results, such as lots of attention or praise, it will be reinforced, and the habit will become even more entrenched. Should the 'Cs' be inhibitive, such as ignoring, the behaviour will tend to fade away, and the habit be broken.

Usually a simple ABC model is presented so that parents can practice observing what comes immediately before and after the target behaviour. If you have not read Chapter 4 on social hearing theory it may be helpful to refer to it to assist in presenting this element of the course. With older children it will often be necessary to examine the distant or past histories to get to the sense of what is happening. This will inform the decisions about what to change in the here and now. For example, one foster daughter persistently refused to have a bath despite all the attempts to persuade her to do so by the foster parents. Having attempted to apply the ABC model the foster parents talked to the social worker about this, and found that the 13-year-old had been sexually abused in the bath some three years previously.

It is also true that some youngsters will have a measure of delayed gratification and this can influence the way we set about changing things. Examples of this can include young people who might behave in a particular way because they know it will either lead to their brother or sister getting into trouble. Alternatively, it may lead to the teenager's parents either becoming wound up or arguing with each other. It is evident from these examples that it may not be just the immediate, in the here and now pay-offs, which are relevant to an understanding of the sense of the behaviour. Older children can wait and work for pay-offs for their own behaviour that occur at some point in the future.

Triggers and pay-offs

Our experience would be, however, that even for teenagers the most likely understanding of their behaviour will be revealed by starting with the immediate triggers and pay-offs. If these do not seem to give a good understanding then it is preferable to begin to look at more distant triggers and pay-offs. Generally parents seem to benefit most from trying to simplify rather than complicate the explanations of behaviour.

By far the greatest hurdle to overcome is being able to take account of the thoughts and feelings involved. For example, parents who know that the pay-off for the teenager's behaviour is the fact that they are being wound up by it may find it hard not to respond and get angry. However, understanding that relationship is the first step to changing it. How that may take place is dealt with in greater depth in Session 4, when listening and communication skills are practised.

All this is a lot to take in, and I would suggest you either build it up slowly, or only elaborate when parents' responses indicate it is necessary. Using a simple ABC observation is often all parents need to make the changes they require.

The following 'Dilesh' exercise, which could be used as a handout, is one way of developing the theme:

- *Background*   Dilesh is 13 years old and has been with a foster carer for about one year.
- *Situation*   He returns home from school at about 4 pm, gets himself a bowl of cereal and starts watching TV. His foster carer, who is the only other person in the house, comes downstairs and asks him to go and quickly tidy his bedroom once he has finished his cereal. Dilesh finishes his cereal but continues to watch TV. Twenty minutes pass and he has made no move towards his bedroom. His foster carer asks him twice more, stating he has not tidied his bedroom in nearly a week and it is in a terrible mess. Dilesh refuses to move. He loses his temper and shouts and screams that she is always nagging him about his bedroom. The consequence of this is that a big argument breaks out, which lasts for ten minutes. He is threatened with being 'grounded' for the night and that the TV will be turned off. This incenses Dilesh even further and his complaints become louder and more abusive. In sheer desperation his foster carer shouts that she 'can't stand this any more' and that it is 'not worth the hassle'. She storms out of the room and Dilesh continues to watch TV. Later that night he goes out with his friends.
- *Exercise*   First, choose one difficult behaviour that Dilesh displays in this scene; second, identify the 'triggers' or events which immediately precede the behaviour; third, list the 'pay-offs' – consequences which come after the behaviour.

An example of the completed exercise could look like this:

ABC exercise

Antecedents or 'Triggers'	Behaviour – the selected behaviour	Consequences or 'pay offs'
Comes in from school	Refuses to move	Requests to tidy repeated
Eats cereal		Nagging about mess (attention)
Watches TV		Argument breaks out
Is asked to tidy bedroom (once cereal is eaten)		Threats made – he increases abuse (gains control)
		Carer backs down He watches TV and later goes out

This exercise can be followed up with watching some video excerpts (for example, Harry Enfield and Chums, 1997), and perhaps also with further practice at formulating an ABC chart while watching that. The objective is to enable group members to see how such careful observation and ordering of the material helps. It is all too easy to go beyond the evidence and interpret or analyse these situations. What we are suggesting is that the information gleaned from simply watching is more often than not enough, and may be the best material to obtain an understanding of the situation. The skill of using the exercise is not to go beyond the material in the script. Invariably people will be drawn into inferences about the story, or want to know more, even to invent it. That tendency can confuse rather than help.

What is 'normal' behaviour?

The topic regarding what is 'normal' behaviour may be included here after the coffee break, or left until the start of the next session. The reasons for including a discussion on the subject of norms at this stage are:

1   Parents attending groups have been bombarded with a confusing range of advice and expectations from relatives, friends, the media, professionals and other parents. It is, therefore, easy for them to think that there is a 'right' and 'wrong' way to bring up teenagers. It is also easy to lose confidence and feel like a 'failed' or 'bad' parent.

2   There are a vast range of different expectations of teenage behaviour and development among parents, depending upon individual preferences, personalities and the race, culture, gender and sexual orientation of the parent. A child with a disability may also experience different parental expectations.

3   In the light of the above two factors it is helpful to allow parents to reflect on their own expectations and to share these with others. It is likely that this will help some parents to reduce their expectations, where they feel these are too high, while other parents may decide they need to increase their motivation to offer firmer and clearer boundaries to their teenagers. What is most important is that parents are allowed to be the 'experts' on their own teenagers and families, and to come to their own conclusions about any changes they might want to make.

4   It is important to have helped parents to reflect on the changes they might want to make in their teenager's behaviour before they embark on the task of actually attempting to make changes. It is pointless to help parents to attempt to change behaviours that they may decide are not really that worrying. It is easier to tolerate some behaviours than to attempt to change them. Other behaviours that result from a disability, or are not achievable for a child of a particular age, may be extremely difficult, if not impossible, to change.

Therefore, before starting to influence and change behaviour patterns, consideration should be given to the desirability of that course. Is it an ethical thing to attempt? Is it practical? Is the behaviour a passing phase? Is it a developmental stage or part of family or cultural patterns?

The following may assist the discussion about what is normal behaviour. In a group which is working well there may be no need for aids to promote discussion, beyond simply posing the question. The theme we normally pursue is to establish that, in fact, norms can be a fiction. Families and cultures will each have their own different working norms, and the discussions only provide ideas which either encourage acceptance of their own situation or offer incentives and direction to work for changes.

Nonetheless, here is a list of possibly disruptive behaviours which are commonly cited by parents. One way to use this list would be for the parents to underline those behaviours which they think might be worrying enough to warrant attempts to change them. Behaviours that they might expect from teenagers should be ignored.

Possibly disruptive behaviours

Being moody	Being uncooperative	Being argumentative
	Lying	Being fussy about food
Staying out late	Getting drunk	Being obsessed about appearance
Taking drugs	Skipping school	Experimenting with sex
Being untidy	Winding up parents	Being unable to save money
Liking loud music	Wearing scruffy clothes	Behaving badly with friends
Experimenting with same-sex relationships		

The list is used to generate discussion about what would be appropriate to change, and what may just have to be lived with. On p. 114 there is a further list of resources, including videos, audio tapes and books, for generating discussion and providing more detailed information.

In addition to keeping monitoring with the charts, and so on, the home task is to add to the record keeping by building up an ABC observation around a chosen behaviour. Most usually that will begin to generate ideas about change strategies without much more input.

Norms – the influence of social factors

In our groupwork with parents in living with teenagers groups the focus of our work is directed towards parents or carers. However, the beneficiaries of our work are the teenagers themselves. It is very apparent, however, in discussions with parents in groups that the parents of teenagers are only one of a range of influences upon teenage behaviour. This is unlike the situation for parents of younger children where parents are often the central and dominant figures in a young child's life.

An exercise that can be included in Session 2 of the living with teenagers programme (under the heading 'what is normal behaviour?') is to ask parents to list on a flip chart all the influences that might have an impact on their teenager's behaviour. Such a list would probably include: friends, school, magazines and books, television and video, computer games, music, brothers/sisters, fashion adverts, parents, sport, alcohol/drugs, health and appearance and boyfriends/girlfriends. To some degree this is comforting to many parents who, before doing such an exercise, had seen themselves as being solely responsible for their teenager's difficult behaviour.

Resources

Having established that teenagers, as growing and developing young adults, are influenced by, and pressured by, a wide range of outside influences, it is helpful to encourage parents to look at issues such as:

- typical teenage development
- the needs of teenagers
- issues of ethics and rights
- understanding the social pressures to which teenagers are subject.

While we would not claim to have any special expertise in these areas, we have widely explored the literature and resources that can be used in work with parents. We offer a short list of resources that you may find useful as a means of generating or guiding discussions with parents in groups.

Videos

'Teenagers – a survival guide for parents', £4.95, can be obtained from Carlton Television, PO Box 101, London WC2N 4AW. The package includes a booklet with a help directory, and is helpful in focusing on the common 'flash points' between parents and teenagers. It also has a good mix of Asian, African-Caribbean and white participants.

'Harry Enfield and Chums, 1997', £12.99, BBC video. This is available from all video stores. It has good short excerpts of 'Kevin the Teenager'.

Audio tapes

Tapes and accompanying booklets for parents, £8.95 each. Titles include 'Teenagers in the family', 'Teenagers under stress', 'Teenagers and drugs', 'Teenagers and sexuality' and 'Teenagers and step-parents'. Copies may be obtained from: Trust for the Study of Adolescence, 23 New Road, Brighton, East Sussex BN1 1WZ. The 'Teenagers in the family' title is very good on listening and communication, and the 'Teenagers and drugs' title is up to date, balanced and has a good directory of helpful organisations.

Books

Useful reference books on children's rights include:

Thirty years of change for children, edited by Gillian Pugh, National Children's Bureau and Whiting and Birch, 1993.

The Handbook of Children's rights – comparative policy and practice, edited by B. Franklin, Routledge, 1995.

All Equal under the Act? A practical guide to the Children Act for Social Workers National Institute for Social Work, Race Equality Unit, London, 1991.

Focus on Teenagers – Research into Practice, Department of Health, HMSO, London, 1996. A helpful publication on the needs of teenagers, this is based on three research studies.

Within the living with teenagers group programme this material is best used towards the end of Session 2, before parents start looking for strategies for changing behaviour.

9 Influencing behaviour: Sessions 3, 4 and 5

Session 3: increasing desired behaviour

1 **Welcome**

- Brief recap on last week
- Feedback on home task – ABCs (half hour at most).
- Warm-up game: reminiscence session.

2 **Main theme: increasing 'good' behaviour**

- Choosing a positive alternative to the unwanted behaviour.
- In 3s, practice selecting desired behaviour.

3 **Coffee break**

4 **Develop a strategy for change**

- Work in small groups to plan changes to increase desired behaviour – ABC formula.

5 **Use of reinforcers**

- Learning what is rewarding for your teenager.
- Tangible reinforcers /pay-offs: tokens, outings, joint activities.
- Discussion exercise on which works the best.

6 **Home task**

- Practice some positive ways of increasing desired behaviour.
- Give out 'Working Together' booklet.

Session 3: increasing desired behaviour

Selecting to start planning for change by *increasing wanted behaviours* is a very deliberate part of the programme. It also represents a considerable shift from where most people begin. Most parents want to decrease or stop behaviours that trouble them and this usually involves some form of punishing strategy. The concept of working to increase desired behaviours is based on the knowledge that strategies for increasing wanted behaviours are much more fun to be involved in for everybody. They are also more effective and probably have a stronger generalising effect.

A good relaxing warm-up exercise which fits in with this theme is to have a reminiscence session, in which the parents attempt to recall those things in their childhood that encouraged them and provided most enjoyment.

In small groups parents list the items they recall and then share them with the main group. There are usually a great many things held in common: outings, pocket money and other treats. Often new games or names of games also emerge and this can create a lot of amusement within the group. Sometimes parents will actually plan a game they enjoyed when young and ask everyone to join in. It is a chance to recall that it was not necessarily the material things which made the most impression in childhood. Above all, however, this exercise is about rooting enjoyable events in the parents' own experience.

Some care needs to be taken with this type of exercise as it can occasionally bring up very deep memories for some. In one group, a mother was totally thrown by it as she could not remember ever receiving any encouragement or having any fun. When there are such reactions, the other parents are often very supportive, but leaders have to be ready also to give extra time, if needed, to talk through the problems raised. These situations are, in our experience, rare. As a rule the exercise releases a great deal of fun and energy.

Increasing 'good' behaviour

In order to begin the process of working to increase a wanted behaviour, it is necessary for parents to *choose an alternative behaviour* to the one which is troublesome. This is an important but not altogether straightforward skill. We ask parents to practice this in small groups so that they can select an alternative behaviour to the one or several behaviours they would like to reduce. An example we might give would be that if a young person stays out late too often we could suggest that concentration on encouraging them to be in on time is going to be more successful than punishing them for staying out late. The alternative needs to be related to the unwanted behaviour, but be something which cannot be performed at the same time. Increasing an alternative thus reduces opportunity and likelihood that the unwanted behaviour will continue.

The sort of difficulties that parents may have when undertaking this exercise might include the following:

1 Still focusing on the negative – If the behaviour they want to reduce is fighting between brother and sister, a parent may suggest that they want to increase 'not fighting between brother and sister'. This can be turned into a positive by suggesting the parent tries to 'increase cooperation between brother and sister'.

2 Unsuitable alternatives – A parent may suggest an unhelpful alternative. For example, a parent who wanted to reduce 'fire-raising' suggested that an alternative was to encourage 'throwing water on it'. The consequence of encouraging the teenager to throw water could have been more damaging than the fire-raising!

3 Taking on too much at once – The alternative to be increased or encouraged may need to be broken down into manageable parts, which can be encouraged a step at a time. For example, a teenager with a poor school attendance record is unlikely to move to 100% attendance in one step. A parent may find that changing the morning routine of preparing for school may bring improved attendance initially, and then moving on to helping with homework will increase the teenager's confidence in their school performance. Moving at a pace that is likely to be achievable gives good opportunities for praise and attention when good behaviour occurs.

The leaders' role is to guide participants sensitively towards shaping and selecting home tasks that will most likely provide some success.

Develop a strategy

When an alternative behaviour has been chosen, plans to achieve it can be considered. The important thing is to be sure that each person selects their own task and clearly sees the purpose of it.

Group leaders should attempt to relate the ways of increasing desired behaviour to the ABC formula. Without using jargon, it is helpful to show how what comes before and after a desired behaviour can really encourage the desired behaviour to occur and become a well-established pattern. Most successful strategies for change involve looking at changing the triggers and also changing the pay-offs.

To change an unwanted behaviour, such as staying out late, select an alternative to it, that is a behaviour you would like. An alternative could be to encourage coming in on time! The following offers a checklist which can be used to monitor work to increase behaviours.

To increase desired behaviour

1   Before the behaviour: antecedents or triggers
      Expect success (prepare psychologically and practically).
      Give clear instructions – model – negotiate.
      Sound as if you mean it (tone of voice).
      Look as if you mean it (body language).

2   After the behaviour: consequences
      Provide incentives (horses for courses).
      Use token systems.
      Express pleasure and use praise.

3   Always – before, after and during the behaviour
      Use appropriate body language.
      Be accurate and use appropriate communication.

From the use of this checklist, a parent in a group came to recognise that whenever she asked her two sons to do anything she would shout at them. Her tone of voice was an exasperated bellow as opposed to a calm and confident request. When she made a change to her approach she was amazed to find she had two reasonably cooperative sons who no longer needed their earplugs!

Looking further at the use of praise, already mentioned in the list above, we refer parents to some guidelines. These offer the following ideas about the most effective use of praise, which include the fact that praise should be:

- Offered as soon as possible after the behaviour has occurred.
- To start with, offered every time the behaviour occurs.
- Given even when other rewards are used.
- Offered with a clear indication of what the praise is for.
- Kept sincere and interesting by the words being changed.
- Offered for good behaviour even if it happens when teenagers have been difficult all day about other things.

This aspect of the programme and the following exercise on pay-offs, are reinforced in cartoon form in pages 5 and 6 of the 'Working Together' booklet, which is given to parents at the end of this session.

Use of reinforcers

Parents are asked to suggest what they think are the most effective reinforcers or pay-offs by ranking the following:

- Money, material goods, games, etc.
- Shared activities, trips out, going swimming, etc.
- Praise, hugs, smiles, attention or 'well done'!

Parents rank them very commonly in the order they are in above, which is, unfortunately, the opposite order of effectiveness. However, this exercise does prompt a lively discussion.

Often *the range of possible reinforcers or pay-offs* is less than obvious. This is especially the case if parent/teenager relations have reached the point where parents will say 'I feel I don't know him/her anymore'. For this reason, we introduce and discuss ways and means of discovering what young people find genuinely rewarding. It needs to be done sensitively and imaginatively, bearing in mind that what is rewarding to one person may not be so to another. Carers can think they are offering incentives, when the sense to the young person is quite different. Getting the meaning across to the young person requires empathy and respect for their wishes and values. One young man was offered outings to the local baths, which he felt he should accept because the family liked to go swimming. In fact he hated it and would have preferred to go bike riding which the others liked less.

In order to promote this search we use a 'like and dislike questionnaire' which asks teenagers to rate a variety of activities, foods and feelings on a scale of zero to five. (Full details of the questionnaire are available from the Centre.)

If this is used as a game it can produce useful information. Many parents have reported delight with it. This is partly because it has given them a way to reopen communication, and partly because they have realised that there are many things their teenagers like, which they did not know about.

The home task for parents between Sessions 3 and 4 is usually best generated by parents working in small groups for the last 15 minutes of the session, to plan ways they can attempt to increase desired behaviour during the coming week. A further home task is to read the 'Working Together' booklet.

Session 4: communication in parent/teenager relationships

1 **Welcome**

- Recap on last week.
- Feedback on increasing desired behaviour.

2 **Main theme: improving communication**

- Skills of listening and communicating.

3 **Practising listening skills**

- Use of role-play to demonstrate difficulties in listening and ways of improving relationships through careful listening.
- Giving parents opportunities to practise and rehearse strategies.
- 'Good' listening checklist (handout).

4 **Coffee break**

5 **Problem-solving and negotiation**

- Looking at ways of resolving disputes and disagreements.
- Introducing the concept of using written agreements.

6 **Home tasks**

- Practising listening, problem-solving and negotiating skills, in order to continue to increase desired behaviour.

Session 4: communication in parent/teenager relationships

Improving communication

With teenagers and older children, issues cannot be resolved unless a fairly *good level of communication* exists. The whole process of increasing desired behaviour involves giving clear messages as well as rewards for agreed performance. That implies not only that the words are understandable, but that the young person is disposed to pay some attention to them. With the older young people it is useful to make some kind of mutual agreement. All of these plans depend upon parents and teenagers talking to each other.

There is not time to practice everything, so we select the most important elements which often get lost when there is conflict (see Chapter 5, 'Resolving family conflict').

The aim is to incorporate practising 'listening' into a role-play. This can be very difficult to do, but is far more effective than simple instruction. It sounds obvious, but actually doing it requires tenacity and restraint, as the natural tendency seems to be to react to what we hear, rather than weigh it up and acknowledge its significance.

One way of achieving this is to use the following scenario to act out as a role-play. (Simon could easily be replaced by Simone – the role-play is not gender-specific.)

> Simon is 14 years old and lives with his parents and a brother and sister both younger than himself. There is constant arguing and shouting in the household. Simon feels Mum and Dad are always 'getting' at him. One Saturday he goes to a disco in town. His parents have agreed he can stay out until 11pm as he will be able to get home on the last bus. He has a great time with his mates, so much so that he forgets to check the time. He has no watch, and when he eventually asks the time he is shocked to discover he has missed the last bus. Simon and his friend know their parents will go mad when they get home. They have no alternative but to walk. To add to their misery it starts to rain. Simon arrives home wet, tired and aching and very scared to face his parents. They are waiting for him …

This scene is acted out initially by group leaders; the purpose of it is to show what so often happens in situations of family conflict, as referred to in Chapter 5. In summary, the task of the group leaders is to act as parents who will do the following things:

● Raise their voices to higher and higher levels.
● Say angry and hurtful things.
● Go off the point and bring in all sorts of past events.
● Not listen to what the teenager is saying.

Such reactions usually produce anger and tension. Parents have also found it helpful if, in the course of the role play, the parents finish up arguing with each other. Parents will often say after this role play, 'That is exactly what we do!' When asked if this works for them they usually say, 'No, but I don't know how to stop myself doing it!'

'Good' listening checklist

A handout lists the following suggestions as a checklist to aid discussion. As communication skills are complex, and when conflict arises they seem to suffer, it is useful to try to practice the following selected skills.

When listening try to achieve the following:

- Give the other person time to say what they feel without being interrupted.
- Try not to react but just listen.
- Use non-verbal encouragement, such as nods and grunts, and maintain eye contact.
- Check that you have got the story right, and check the accuracy of your own understanding (ask, 'did you say' – 'is that right?')
- Try to show you have noticed the feelings involved (ask, 'you seem upset' – 'tired?')
- Try to avoid becoming angry, and just reacting; it will make matters worse and make it impossible for you to listen to them or them to hear you.

The following could be added to the listening skills above, but take care not to make the exercises too complex. So although we do mention expressing positive feelings and also negative ones, to achieve assimilation of all this in one evening could be too much. The basis of it all is the listening, so be sure that is not skimmed over.

Expressing positive feelings

Look at the person and try to let your body language match your feelings. Say exactly what they did which pleased you. Tell the person how it made you feel.

Expressing negative feelings

Look at the person, speak firmly and let your body language match your mood. Tell the other person exactly what they did that upset you. Tell them how it made you feel clearly, but as calmly as possible. Suggest ways to avoid future upsets and also suggest alternatives to the upsetting patterns. Reassure the person that it is the behaviour that bothers you, and that you still love/regard them highly.

These suggestions can be used as checklists to help make a note of what goes wrong – or well – as the role-play develops. Hopefully, parents will re-enact the scene using the skills listed. If they are too shy, a definite second-best is to discuss what should have been done. It is very easy to talk about how skills were used in retrospect, but more difficult and more useful to actually practice using them.

The home task could include a plan with deliberate attempts to start to work for change, which could be worked on and shaped in small groups during the last part of the session. For example, it could be that tokens or some other scheme of reinforcement are adopted, to, for example, encourage the completion of homework on time. However, if the problem is more difficult, a preliminary may just be to start practising listening and discovering what the young person likes. In the latter case, just practising listening and creating ABCs would be an adequate home task.

Some parents may want to progress to the concept of using written agreements, as described at the end of Chapter 5; for others this may take a little longer and can be developed within a response cost programme as outlined at the end of Session 5.

Session 5: changing unwanted behaviour – sanctions that work

1 Welcome

- Feedback.
- Recap on last week.
- Warm-up: reminiscence session – punishments.

2 Main theme: strategies to reduce unwanted behaviour

- Problems with these.

3 Techniques

- Ignoring
- Removing privileges
- Reparation
- Response cost programmes.

4 Coffee break

5 Negotiating and compromising with teenagers

- Creating ideas exercise (brainstorming).
- Response cost (handout).

6 Devising 'response cost' programmes

7 Home task

- Consider and attempt to involve teenager(s) in change plan, bringing all the skills and techniques into play.

8 Remind parents to bring a blanket and cushion next week for relaxation.

Session 5: changing unwanted behaviour – sanctions that work

A useful warm-up activity is to repeat the reminiscence session, but this time focus on punishments of which parents were themselves on the receiving end. This exercise is best done in small groups. When the feedback to the whole group is undertaken, try to draw out the thinking and feelings which such memories evoke.

This activity anchors the next part of the session firmly in reality. It attempts to consider the disadvantages of 'punitive' strategies, and the care with which they need to be used if relationships are not to be damaged. Teenagers are particularly sensitive to injustice; they need to feel that action taken against them is fair. They may not agree with the punishment at the time, but can later appreciate the need for restraints. Relationships need not be spoiled if, on reflection, the teenager appreciates that their parents were well-intentioned and applied the punishment thoughtfully.

Excessive use of punitive strategies to reduce behaviours have a number of bad side effects. Here are some examples that parents have drawn to our attention:

- Unpleasant to administer
- Unpleasant to receive
- Likely to spoil relationships and make people cross and unhappy
- Physical punishments tend to teach that hitting and aggression is acceptable
- More likely to teach teenagers *not to get caught* rather than not to do it again
- Unhelpful because they do not tell teenagers what parents would like
- Remembered most often as unfair
- Unlikely to work in the long run, but can get used more and more.

There are probably others. The point, however, is not to discount punishments entirely, but to issue them with a strong health warning and ensure that they are only used when well-established, positive encouragements are kept intact.

Techniques in reducing unwanted behaviour

Most parents will be familiar with the main strategies. However, because they will have used punishments without positive strategies, they will have found them to be ineffective.

Selective ignoring

This includes a whole range of responses, from a deliberate walking away to diversion to other subjects. The point of being selective is that a general ignoring will discourage desirable as well as unhelpful behaviours. Care needs to be taken to ensure that the ignoring is deliberate, focused and understood by the young person.

Removal of privileges

The removal of privileges embraces a huge range from grounding to loss of pocket money. It seems to be essential to ensure the removals are balanced and fair, not too extreme, and practical in so far as parents can keep to what they say. Another facet to consider is that denial of good things can create an atmosphere of no hope for both parents and teenager. One parent denied their teenager attendance at youth club as a punishment. In fact, it was about the only leisure activity which the lad had in which he received real encouragement and acknowledgement. The respite and other advantages the family were getting from this club were considerable, as he was more relaxed and amiable when he attended. Denying him access to the club hurt everybody and achieved nothing. It is so important to keep something worthwhile in place for everybody's sake.

Reparation

This describes the concept of teenagers putting right whatever they have done wrong. This might include: clearing up if they have made a mess, repairing something they have broken, or paying for something they have damaged. It is important that 'the punishment fits the crime', and if the teenager can suggest the reparation they feel is reasonable, then they are more likely to do it without the whole exercise leading to bad feelings all round.

'Time out' is a form of punishment that is rarely used with teenagers, although for some younger teenagers it may be useful. However, by the time most children have become teenagers they are likely to put their parents in time out! In work with teenagers it is often more helpful to suggest to parents that they take time out – for example, by locking themselves in the loo! This gives a parent time to calm down and think and it can also be used to ignore difficult behaviour, if that behaviour is getting a pay-off from the excessive parental attention it receives. After having time to think, a parent may be able to try to encourage more positive alternative behaviour. [If this is a strategy you feel might be appropriate, it is described in detail in our other book *Promoting Positive Parenting* (1995, p. 98).]

Response cost programmes

These are programmes that teach the principle that an individual's actions have consequences within their own control. Antisocial behaviour bears a cost to themselves, and acceptable behaviour can earn rewards. The programme described below is an example of this. It is a combination of negotiating agreements, positive encouragements (hugs, praise, smiles and material rewards), and the removal of some privileges for identified unacceptable behaviour. This response cost programme relies *heavily* on the use of tokens.

- Use a small notebook. Keep this where the participant can see it to check progress.
- Keep the first few pages for the rules and the subsequent changes to them, for example, the first page may look like this:

John's agreement

1. If John comes home before 11.00 pm, then he will receive 2 tokens each night.
2. Whenever John comes home before 11.00pm, for 3 successive nights, then he will receive a bonus of 5 extra tokens.
3. The tokens will be given as near to the event as possible. Praise and encouragement will be given as the token is put in the book.
4. Tokens cannot be taken back in any circumstances. Only bonus tokens can be removed.
5. When enough tokens are collected, they can be exchanged for any item in the 'menu'.

- A 'menu' can be written at the back of the notebook and can consist of any items, however fantastic, which the participant would really like (it does not mean they will get it!!). A trade-in value in the number of tokens is given to each item. John's 'menu' was like this:

Trip to Cinema	10	Trip to Disneyland	2,000,000
Disco	50	2 friends for tea	10
Theme Park	300	Swimming	5
New Trainers	400	Stop up 1hr extra	5

He could add to it as he chose, while the allocation of tokens was at his parents' discretion.

- The record of progress is important. John's daily record looked like this:

	Home by 11 pm	Tokens	Bonus tokens	Total tokens
Monday	Yes	2		2
Tuesday	Yes	2		2
Wednesday	Yes	2	5	11
Thursday	NO	0		11
Friday	Yes	2		13
Saturday	Yes	2		15
Sunday	Yes	2	5	22
Total weekly		12	10	22
Total carried forward to next week				22

- Giving additional tokens as a bonus is very effective in increasing the young person's sense of achievement. It can be seen from the above agreement that John earned 12 tokens for coming home on time (two per day). His bonus provided ten extra tokens, almost as much again as he earned. His lapse on the Thursday meant that he fell short of an even greater number of tokens.
- Removing tokens should not be encouraged, because if it is done too freely, then the young person will lose enthusiasm and the incentive to try hard will reduce. However, a cost element can be introduced, but this must be written into the agreement. This consists of removing bonus points only as a penalty.
- So, for example, it was added to John's agreement later that he could loose one bonus point, but no others, every time he hit his sister.
- Important ground rules to remember:

    1) Ensure that there is good and fair negotiation with your teenager.
    2) Remember to listen to your teenager.
    3) Ensure that your teenager never loses more than he/she earns.
    4) Only remove bonus points.

5) Show enthusiasm for the programme and reward and praise your teenager for every small achievement.
6) Be prepared to change the programme, or add to it, in order to help the process.
7) Do not be drawn into agreeing to expensive items in the 'menu'. There will be plenty of items that teenagers enjoy that do not cost a lot of money.
8) Try to make the programme as much 'fun' as possible.

Negotiating and compromising with teenagers

An advantage of this kind of scheme is that it can be used with all the young people in a family, if necessary, to avoid the criticism that the focus is on the one who creates the problems. All the children can be involved in getting tokens even if there is no great problem with their behaviour. One lad refused to join in until he saw his siblings enjoying the scheme. He then decided he was foolish to miss out on the rewards available, and a very serious problem of hitting and throwing was overcome.

Important principals of problem-solving are incorporated into the above programme, as the process involves generating as many ideas as possible which might contribute towards a solution. In the menu the 'Trip to Disneyland' would be beyond the reach of most families, so it has to be managed by realistic pricing in tokens.

Letting everybody say what they would like, however fantastic, seems to bring in that important fun element, which hopefully will also generate useful alternatives as well. From among the ideas, which can perhaps be written on a large piece of paper, it is then possible to erase those ideas which are either impractical or which might make things even worse. This can be a preliminary to genuine negotiation about which ideas are acceptable to everybody. Obviously it is likely to involve some compromise, but it should move towards workable solutions as courses of action are agreed upon.

Designing a response cost programme

A task for the end of the session could well be to see if a response cost programme applicable to group members' situations could be drafted in fairly realistic terms. Of course it could not be completed without the young person, who would have to be involved in the discussions if any such scheme was to work effectively. Parents will have been practising the skills involved in encouraging such discussions and, although they may not all be perfect at this point, most parents attending will have begun to make significant and very heartening progress. By this stage of the group the parents will be familiar with all the available strategies, and their home task would be to continue to bring all these to bear on improving the quality of the relationship with their teenager(s).

At the end of the session, refer to the next session's activities as they may like to wear casual clothes and bring a pillow and blanket with them for the relaxation.

10 Looking after ourselves, evaluation and goodbyes: Sessions 6 and 7

Session 6: looking after ourselves

Session 6: looking after ourselves

1 **Welcome**

- Recap last week.
- Feedback (20 to 30 minutes).

2 **Different ways of relieving stress and tension**

- Ways for parents of 'looking after themselves'.
- Ways that help parents identify and learn to cope with personal stress and tensions.
- Support Groups. Parents encouraged to think about forming their own support groups once the course has finished.

3 **Thoughts and feelings**

- How our thoughts and feelings can effect the way that we behave – triangle of influences.
- Brief introduction to cognitive behavioural therapy and simple ways to begin to understand thoughts and feelings.

4 **Coffee break**

5   **Practical exercises on relaxation**

- How parents can 'look after themselves' and learn how to cope with stress.
- Practising relaxation techniques with either a parent leading the exercises, or using the Centre's relaxation tape.

6   **Reminder to the parents that next session is the last one – and to bring goodies to the 'party'.**

By this stage in the course the feedback should flow quite readily and so it is important to allow sufficient time for parents to share their personal thoughts and feelings. Probably at least twenty minutes, and no more than thirty minutes, would be adequate. We find that parents are by this time recapping and fine tuning their work, or some may even be at the point of wanting the discussions to range over a wider field of topics.

This session has proved to be often one of the most rewarding and telling sessions in the whole programme. Rita Naag (1997), who researched one of our groups, queried whether it should come first because her work showed that people who felt most positive about themselves did best. She also noted that, without exception, parents really appreciated the confirmation that they should look after their own needs and had a right to do so. This is exactly what this session encourages. However, our experience over the last seven years suggests that progress in looking after oneself and being more positive is also very much enhanced by the work done on managing young people's behaviour. We think it might be a little heavy to start such a short course dealing with deeper personal issues and, therefore, it is more appropriate to leave this work until Session 6, when parents are more relaxed and know and trust each other much more. It appears that the theme of this session is emphasised more by leaving the work they have been doing with their teenagers entirely to one side and concentrating on themselves. However, it is important to recognise that a calm and confident parent will be more able to deal effectively with the task of improving their relationship with their teenager than a stressed, burnt-out, ranting and raving adult who responds to every event like a tightly coiled spring or a dormant volcano.

Different ways of relieving stress and tension

Two possible ways can be used to present this part of the session. First, it can be helpful to ask the participants to think about how they recognise when they are under stress. This can be done by asking what the physical symptoms might be or what might stress do to their coping mechanisms.

Another way of starting is to invite small groups of participants to explore or fantasise what they would like to do or have for themselves. There can be no predicting what will come out, but a common theme is that people want time and space for themselves away from the young people and the chores of everyday life. The findings are shared in the large group. This is a good time to mention or repeat the idea of forming a support group among themselves. Quite often the parents will have already begun to think of doing this themselves, as they are already feeling mutual support from the group. They may want books, or information about evening classes, or ask you to help them arrange some instruction for an extended or completely new group.

In this session there is opportunity to use your own particular skills and local knowledge to create links for the future, or wind the group down to finish on a constructive note. It is important that parents are helped to recognise their own skills and potential. Simply ask them what they find useful for relieving stress and tension. Often some very imaginative ideas are shared. Some may offer to lead part of the session. One parent demonstrated some simple yoga exercises to the group. If you are lucky, there may be an aromatherapist within the group but if not simply burning some relaxing essential oils sets the atmosphere and helps enormously.

Thoughts and feelings

We use part of the time in this session to present models which can be helpful in dealing with stress and making life more enjoyable. We then suggest that the work done so far has focused specifically on changing behaviour. By way of introduction this illustration can be used:

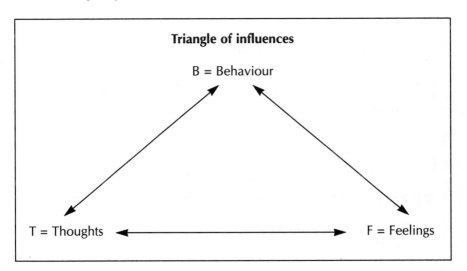

Triangle of influences

B = Behaviour

T = Thoughts

F = Feelings

The diagram shows that there is a relationship between *behaviour, thoughts and feelings*, and that problems we experience can be manifest in other ways than *just* behaviour. The problems are very directly influenced by what we feel – if we are feeling ill, or angry, or profoundly sad. Sometimes these feelings make it difficult to get on with work, or react socially as we normally would. We may behave untypically and sometimes be immobilised until we have regained our composure.

Thinking also can affect the way we behave, and the way we feel. What we try to do is to provide parents with a simple but useful acquaintance with cognitive behavioural ideas. These provide important concepts to help deal with the powerful influence that thinking can have over both behaviour and feelings. However, we would not refer to it as 'cognitive behavioural therapy' in the group, and would introduce the idea of 'the stories we tell ourselves'.

In the session we use a grid to encourage discussion regarding the interplay of *feelings – thoughts – and behaviour*. Examples personal to ourselves or group members can be included if that seems appropriate. The process can be developed in the following sequence:

1 Think of an event that is commonly most stressful to you and put it in the first column.

Event	thought	feeling	outcome
teenager out late			

2 Now try to recall how such an event makes you feel!

Event	thought	feeling	outcome
teenager out late		anxious and worried	

3 What story might you have been telling yourself as this was going on?

Event	thought	feeling	outcome
teenager out late	she's at a rave – will take ecstacy	anxious and worried	

4 Can we predict what the outcome might be? A possibility would be:

Event	thought	feeling	outcome
teenager out late	she's at a rave – will take ecstacy	anxious and worried	will question teenager anxiously – be inclined not to believe them

Most group members will be able to identify with something like this, or produce their own scenarios which trouble them. The usefulness of this is that just as we spent some time identifying carefully which behaviours to change, similarly we can change our thinking. By identifying which stories we tell ourselves that are habitually unhelpful, we recognise triggers to uncomfortable feelings and can take evasive action.

Up until now in the group, we have looked for behaviour patterns to change. At this point we now help parents to look for thought patterns which may warrant change. Where this fits an individual's experience they can move on to generate alternatives to the unhelpful thoughts. The four grids above can therefore be extended as follows:

5 Parents can identify what might be a more helpful thought or way to respond to the situation, and put this in the second row of the following table:

Event	thought	feeling	outcome
teenager out late	she's at a rave – will take ecstacy	anxious and worried	will question teenager anxiously – be inclined not to believe them
	I don't like raves but she has been fairly sensible in the past		

6 Such a thought creates a different feeling. Instead of feeling worried to distraction it stirs more positive feelings. The result could then be:

Event	thought	feeling	outcome
teenager out late	she's at a rave – will take ecstacy	anxious and worried	will question teenager anxiously – be inclined not to believe them
	I don't like raves but she has been fairly sensible in the past	less anxious more trustful	ask the teenager if they enjoyed themselves

It is worth working through several examples, and dealing with the questions which arise. One parent found she had always assumed that having a child meant her own needs had always to come second. She realised that, for her own and the young person's sake, she needed some time alone and he needed to learn that it was important not to expect that she danced to his every whim! Obviously, in the time available, this is only a very brief introduction to these concepts, which may enthuse people sufficiently to want further information. This discussion should take you through to coffee.

Practical exercises for relaxation

After coffee, we talk briefly about how individuals cope with stress. Sometimes a member of the group is present who does yoga, or something similar, who could introduce or lead the relaxation. It is best to have completed all the work of the evening before starting the relaxation, so that people can go home feeling the most benefit from just winding down in that way. Make sure all notices or reminders have been given before this point.

We have a tape available if you are not confident enough, at first, to lead the exercise yourself. The point we want to make is that, with practice, we can all learn to have some control and quite quickly alleviate the worst effects of anxiety and stress as they occur.

The relaxation exercises on the tape we have produced includes examples of various techniques.

In the session we offer only a taste of a small range of relaxation techniques. This is done by using a sequence which includes muscle relaxation, deep breathing and meditation. Any of these could be taken to much higher levels of expertise than we have time for in the group session. The idea is to provide a choice, so that participants can select what will individually suit them best.

The tape dwells on the theme of sand and beaches. Obviously this will not suit everybody. However, there are various other themes such as water, wind, music, bird-song, and all are available on commercial tapes.

Here is an excerpt from our tape:

> Before you begin it is important that you're comfortable. So perhaps just stretch out your legs in front of you – wiggle yourself into a comfortable position on your chair, or if you prefer, lie stretched out on the floor. After this brief practice you should not feel you have to rush away to the next task, so once the talking stops, allow yourself to come back into the room and to the other people, in your own time, no matter what others may be doing.
>
> Now, first of all we will practise realising the level of control we can have over our own bodies, and the tension that develops in it from time to time.
>
> To do this, I would like you to hold an arm out in front of you. Then clench your fist as tightly as you can, making the finger nails dig into the palm. At the same time, push the arm forward, feeling it stretch and strain and quiver.
>
> Now ... let it go! Let your arm rest limply on your lap or by your side, and tease out the fingers, wriggling and loosening them. And feel the difference! Register the difference! And realise that, when we get anxious, our bodies tense up like that, but also realise that if we are aware of it, we can, with practice, let go.
>
> Try just one more exercise.
>
> This time tighten up your face, clench your teeth, press them together really hard so that you feel the muscles of your jaw strain. Screw up your eyes so that you furrow your forehead into a tight frown, straining the muscles round the forehead and cheeks almost to aching point. And now ... let it go!

Shake your head…
  Soften your eyes…
    If you can, let your forehead relax.
It may not be possible, but nonetheless, feel the difference, your face more relaxed and comfortable. Make sure that your teeth are not together but slightly apart; your lips also could be slightly open. Notice how your breath moves, naturally, quietly, just as your body wants it to. Notice the difference!
  We will move on now to concentrate a little more specifically on our breathing.
  What I would like you to do is to notice the tip of your nose, just concentrate on the tip of your nose. When you breathe in, notice the air passing through your nose:

IN (breathe deeply)   OUT (exhale firmly)
IN   OUT

Just notice the air coming in from the outside filling your body with life and energy and peace. Then lay back so that you are one with the life around and in you. Notice the breathing, and be aware of it going

IN   OUT

It doesn't matter if your mind wanders, but try to keep bringing it back to the breathing and letting the air course in and out, slowly, slowly caressing your nose! You will notice you relax more and more:

IN (deep breath in)   OUT (firmly exhale)
IN   OUT

Now to build up a scene in your imagination, marry this IN and OUT of the air passing your nose to the tide lapping gently IN and OUT on a beach of soft golden sand. Spread your towel on the sand, and put down any packs; take off any tight clothes. Lie down and feel the weight of your body being carried by the sand, sand that shifts, as you wriggle, to make a comfortable custom-made bed.
  You are relaxing, feeling your arms resting on the sand, and your fingers playing with the soft tickling sand. Your back is supported and comfortable, your chest rises and falls … slowly, and yet more slowly. Your eyes become softer, heavier and softer, and still the air is coursing past the tip of your nose with great IN (suck in a breath)

and OUT (push out a breath)
so slowly IN and OUT.

All of this links with the rhythm of the sea, still gently lapping, you notice your bottom comfortably supported but wriggle to make it even more so, more and more comfortable. You thighs and calves are supported by the sand.
  You raise one leg. Then feel your foot push into the sand caressing the soft silky grains. You and your body are one with the world around you, this beautiful, warm, encouraging, restful world.
  Still your breathing gets slower and calmer and your nose notices everything! as the air comes IN and OUT.

You hear the surf, scent the hibiscus at the beach's edge, you sense and see, in your mind's eye, the soft rustling of the palms there. Your body feels heavier and heavier pressing snugly into the sand. With your own rhythm, settle down and relish all this (you don't need my words now) let your own imagination catch everything that comes in on your breath

IN through your nose
OUT through your nose

quietly ... restfully ... blissfully ...

Without knowing it, you are charging your batteries – quietly the energy of the sea, and the wind and your heart is filling you, replenishing you, to make you fresh and full of energy and peace and hope ...

I will stop talking and let you decide when, in your own time, to return to this room and this company.

The group then breaks up in its own time to say farewells or simply disperse.

Session 7: evaluation and goodbyes

Session 7: evaluation and goodbyes

1   Welcome

- Feedback.

2   'Troubleshooting'

- This is for parents who may still be having difficulties with their young people, to have some additional time to iron out any remaining problems.

3   Evaluation feedback: of presenters and of the group

- The Teenage Behaviour and Communication Rating Scale (see Appendix A) is repeated, and the overall results presented to the parents, showing the degree of change that hopefully has occurred during the course.

4   Social activity for the evening

5   Saying goodbyes

The seventh session is mainly a social occasion, providing an opportunity for people to mark the end of the group. It usually takes place two to three weeks after Session 6, to allow parents to work by themselves while the safety net of one more session is available. They may wish to be sure that plans for a support group are set in place. The most successful ideas usually come from parents themselves; they can offer the most practical and apposite suggestions for their own locality.

'Troubleshooting'

Although the majority of the time in this final session is for social activity, there may be parents who need a little extra help and support, and usually there is the time in this final session to do this. Only occasionally have we found it necessary for a parent to want further individual help, and obviously if this happens, time constraints in your agency will determine this. We have never had a parent who has come back for a second living with teenagers group, but we are not quite sure how to analyse this! However, we do encourage parents who are interested to come to future groups to assist other parents and talk about their experiences. We find this a most effective way of empowering people, and it also helps parents on new groups to relax more, knowing that parents have come back to talk of their experiences.

Evaluation feedback: of presenters and of the group

The evaluation includes filling in a second questionnaire, which is a repeat of the Centre's rating scale done as a preliminary to Session 1. This can then provide a 'before and after' profile showing the degree of change the parents feel have occurred in their young people's behaviour. It might be helpful to make an anonymous graph of this data or just a simple bar chart on a flipchart paper showing this. Clearly, if one member was struggling and the results would be an embarrassment to them, it would be best not to use it immediately. For future groups and home visits to parents who wish to have information about the success rate of the groups, such visual evidence is easily understood and gives powerful encouraging messages. Remember to collect and feed back to participants as many different indicators of success as possible. Anecdotal material – 'Mrs ... said she had seen you looking so much better' – and simple but accurate observations, can all enhance the sense of achievement and well-being for parents, which is what we hope to achieve.

It is also useful to know how the course and the presenters were judged; the comments can help shape up future presentations. Again, more information about evaluation is to be found in Chapter 11 on that subject.

Social activity and goodbyes!

The main objective of this final session is farewells and feedback. Parents usually choose themselves how they would like to spend the time, which can range from going to the local pub to everyone bringing some food and drink to share in the venue where the group has been running. People become quite emotional when saying goodbye at the end of the group. Quite often parents admit that they have never shared so many personal feelings with other parents before, and therefore some close support friendships have build up. However, a support group has usually been arranged by this stage, so although the living with teenagers group has finished, there is also the feeling of a new beginning to something else. This can be very empowering for parents, as it will be something they are setting up for themselves to organise and run in whatever way they choose. Quite often, we get invited back for a social event, which is very heartwarming for us!

Recently we have given certificates for attending the course (see Appendix C), and these can be offered with some ceremony and, if people so wish, some photographs taken. We feel that attention to all these details leads to positive endings for all concerned.

Part IV

Follow-up after the group

11 Evaluation

How to evaluate: measures and indicators

Why is it important to evaluate?

For many practitioners the notion of evaluation can appear threatening and time-consuming. The Centre believes it to be both positive and constructive. The following points argue strongly that, with minimum effort, evaluation can be both time- and cost-effective.

- Evaluation means gathering information, data or evidence which can be used to measure effectiveness. It can also have applications in the setting of standards and gives the 'user' an opportunity to have a say about the quality of service.
- Evaluation is about partnership and cooperation between clients and practitioners. It is a dynamic and on-going process in which many lessons can be learned about needs and appropriate responses.
- We cannot assume that intervention has been effective, either with individual casework or groupwork. Therefore, success or failure can only be gauged if clear measures are established beforehand.
- Good planning, whereby clear goals and targets are negotiated, facilitates evaluation and saves time in the long run.
- Evaluation must play a crucial role in meeting the objectives of the Children Act and establishing good working practices.
- Evaluation increases effectiveness and the quality of practice because it provides both the evidence for success and the reasons why interventions can go wrong.

- Clients should expect and deserve an effective evaluated service which meets their needs.
- Evaluation gives clear evidence to higher management that using these behavioural approaches in a thorough and effective manner does show extremely good research-based results. This demonstrates a very cost-effective process in the long run, it provides concrete evidence that the groupwork programme does help parents and avoids family breakdown.

The evaluation process

The following flow chart or model, informs the Centre's groupwork approach with parents, in both living with teenagers and fun and families groups. The model demonstrates the dynamic and fluid nature of the evaluation process. Measuring effectiveness is not always the final stage as it can lead to renegotiation of objectives in problem explanation. As with the Children Act, partnership, negotiation and involvement are central elements.

The evaluation process

Negotiation of measurable objectives

↓

Assessment Establishing a baseline Review progress and original objectives

↓

Generate a hypothesis or explanation of the problem

↓

Negotiate intervention Test out explanation

↓

Monitor/record progress over agreed period of time

↓

Evaluate effectiveness

How should I evaluate?

In setting up and running a group, or carrying out individual work, it is important to decide what you are measuring and why you are doing so. In our groupwork programme for parents of teenagers there are a number of measurable elements:

- Frequency and number of teenage behaviour difficulties reported by parents
- Improvements in listening and communication skills of parents
- Parental reported improvement and progress in the 'target' behaviours
- Parental satisfaction with each session and the progress as a whole
- Parental thoughts, feelings and beliefs (primarily for research study purposes)
- Parent-child interaction within the natural home environment. (primarily for research study purposes).

How to measure

The following seven measuring devices have been used in our groupwork programmes.

Teenage Behaviour Inventory   Approximately one to three weeks before the beginning of the groupwork programme, all the parents are visited at home. They are asked to complete a Teenage Behaviour and Communication Rating Scale. This is designed to measure the frequency and number of teenage behaviour problems and the quality of communication between parents and teenagers. It provides valuable baseline or assessment data which gives a benchmark to measure change. Male or female partners are asked to complete the questionnaire independently. This sometimes illustrates large discrepancies between partners in two-parent families.

During Session 7, parents reflect on the programme as a whole. They complete the same questionnaire as they filled in prior to Session 1 and the two papers are compared in order to find out if change has occurred. The aim is to assess parents' reported changes in their teenagers' communication and behaviours from the beginning to the end of the course. There is a 'troubleshooting' session at the final meeting in order to deal with any remaining problems and to assess if progress has been maintained over a greater length of time.

Tracking and recording   The first two sessions aim to equip parents with the necessary skills to systematically define, track and record teenage behaviour. This recording is continued throughout the seven sessions which are detailed in Part III of the book. The recording will demonstrate if the behaviour increases or decreases. It provides an indicator by which to judge whether or not the objectives a person wants are being achieved. Keeping diaries and a 'typical day' account is also useful.

Observation In order to gauge directly the level of behavioural difficulties and the quality of parent-teenager interaction, a series of role-play techniques are employed. These exercises focus particularly on the way requests are made to teenagers and the ability to praise the achievement of specific tasks and to ignore behaviours that might be just very irritating.

Time sampling This is a method of recording which enables data to be gathered for specific periods of the day. It is particularly useful if parents feel overwhelmed or they may be inconsistent in their record-keeping. An example would be where tracking and recording showed that the highest frequency of a problem behaviour occurred at meal times. Therefore, a parent may wish to choose just dinner time as the specific period for time sampling.

Graphs These display the frequency of events or behaviour through simple line graphs. They visibly chart the level of progress from assessment stage through to intervention. Quite often parents 'feel' there is no improvement in their child's behaviour, so by seeing the improvement in a simple graph, they feel more reassured and confident.

Cognition and emotional feelings In Session 5 and Chapter 6 the role of cognitive work is described. Parents' feelings often change dramatically during the course of the group. Cognitive behaviour therapy indicates the importance of measuring thought processes and their impact on the way a person feels and behaves. Understanding cognitive blocks can be important when dealing with parents who get stuck and feel unable to carry out practical tasks. Simple rating scales, such as 0 to 5, or 0 to 100, can be employed when monitoring the strength of specific thoughts. These thoughts can include how bad a person feels and the emotional intensity of the situation. Examples can be seen in Chapter 8 of the strong feelings and the contrast in comments made at the beginning and towards the end of a group.

Video and audio recording The use of video and audio recording as, 'fly on the wall' techniques, can be extremely powerful for measuring patterns of interaction and communication. They can be helpful when working with people who have reading and writing difficulties, and can also be a very effective means of recording teenage communication.

Evaluation of the Centre's results

During the past four years the Centre for Fun and Families have continuously evaluated their work with both individual families and the groupwork programmes along lines outlined earlier in this chapter. Below are a series of tables which give the results from evaluating the groups.

Results from evaluating living with teenagers groups

The table below shows an overall evaluation of a group run in 1996. The results are typical of other groups run in a four-year period.

Overall group evaluation

How well was the course organised and presented?	Range 3–5	Mean 4.12
How well were the practical elements explained and demonstrated?	Range 3–5	Mean 4.12
Were the topics covered in sufficient depth?	Range 3–5	Mean 4.25
What level of progress do you feel you have made since the course started?	Range 2–5	Mean 3.50
What level of support and help did you receive from the other parents?	Range 2–5	Mean 4.00
Did the sessions demand too much or too little from you? Circle '0' if about right, a minus number if too little, a positive number if too much.	Range –1–0	Mean 4.00

Key: 0 = very poor, 1 = poor, 2 = fair, 3 = good, 4 = very good, 5 = excellent.

The group illustrated in the evaluation took place in January/February 1996. The results are significantly high and are typical of other groups run throughout a four-year period. Six questionnaires were completed and there was one dropout during the course of the group.

The list of comments below shows typical parental feedback at completion of a seven-week living with teenagers programme:

- 'To be able to stand back and take a more detached view of our behaviour and our son's was helpful, as was being with others with similar situations.'
- '(The group leaders) listened to each of us and did not pass any judgement on us. We found that this group helped us both, with support, advice and we also found help meeting with other members of our group.'
- 'Taking time to listen has been important to us and learning to control our behaviour has made a big difference.'
- 'We began to realise why the group leaders hadn't given us all the answers. There were no simple answers that would work for each and every one of us. The only way to find answers was to try out different suggestions made not only by those running the course but also suggestions by others attending the course.'
- 'Lines of communication that had broken down have been reopened and we no longer feel alone with our problems.'
- 'Looking at ways to change behaviour patterns in our teenagers often led us to change our own behaviour patterns.'
- 'We, I think, like the others, wanted the answers straight away. (The group leaders) said there are many steps to take before solving the behaviour problems and each step will make a difference. This has been true.'

There are many reasons why some parents have limited achievement on the groupwork programmes. Some have to do with the group itself:

- Size of group, above eight or below three
- Poor attendance (though level of actual dropout is small)
- Childcare problems when attending the group.

Some group members have problems with their partners who may be:

- Unsupportive
- Working away from home
- Working shifts or long hours
- Having marital difficulties.

Some single-parent group members experience a lack of social support.
   Group members cited problems with their children as reasons for limited progress:

- Long-standing teenage behaviour problems
- Confusion and lack of consistency in teenage behaviour management

- Long-standing patterns of negative parent-teenager interaction (centred on punishment and control).

Finally, some parents attain limited results from the group because of a lack of belief in positive change or because of chaotic family life.

The above lists only represent 'potential' factors why parents do 'less well' on the programme. They should not be used to exclude individuals from attending because many parents join a group because they are experiencing one or more of the above factors. Living with teenagers groups have consistently been shown to be effective over a wide client population, including families where there are acute child protection concerns or the teenagers are at risk of being accommodated. The large majority of parents report a level of positive change. The essential therapeutic elements in running a successful group are listed below:

Logical structure and careful group planning	Empathy and rapport
Step-by-step approach	Keeping on task
Application of principles to individual circumstances	Practising of methods and techniques (within group and at home)
Full parental participation and involvement	Humour and fun
Two group leaders	Weekly 'homework' tasks
Power sharing with strategies for change	Evaluation by parents and group leaders
Weekly recaps of each session	Keeping within time constraints (2 hours per session)
Constant reference to parental examples and own practice	Relating behaviour to social learning theory
Being clear and specific about 'target' or problem behaviour	Negotiating measurable goals and objectives
Encouraging social support between parents and anti-discriminatory practice throughout	Using exercises which reinforce 'team' working/building
Trying to be imaginative and dynamic in approach	Chasing up parents who do not attend, if appropriate
If appropriate, offering individual advice	Ongoing support through support groups

We have found the above to be important for running effective groups. The table below shows the results from a groupwork programme run between January and February 1996:

Teenage behaviour evaluation results

	No. of behaviour problems		No. of communication difficulties	
	Pre-group	Post-group	Pre-group	Post-group
Parent 1	12	15	5	3
Parent 2	14	15	5	6
Parent 3	16	4	5	1
Parent 4	14	4	3	3
Parent 5	5	7	2	0
Parent 6	2	1	4	1
Mean	**63**	**46**	**24**	**14**
reduction		**27%**		**42%**

This table provides evaluation results from the Centre's Teenage Behaviour Evaluation Form, which asks whether each behaviour is currently seen as a problem or not. In addition, the form asks six questions about the parent's perception of communication difficulties. The Evaluation Form also measures the frequency of 19 behaviour difficulties and uses a 1–5 rating scale (never–always).

The figures in the table above demonstrate a significant reduction (27%) in teenage behaviour difficulties and decline of 42% in communication difficulties from the start to the end of the group. Comparatively, the results are similar to other groups that have been held during the last four years. However, when compared to the evaluated outcomes of fun and families groups for parents of younger children (2–12 years), the results appear less positive. Fun and families groups have consistently achieved an average of 50% reductions in child behaviour difficulties, whereas living with teenagers groups seem to average a lower 30% reduction. Yet the parents attending living with teenagers groups seem to be equally positive and satisfied with their progress and their comments reflect this. For example, the comments from a group of Asian fathers of teenagers meeting during January/February 1996 included the following:

- 'Made me realise that other parents face similar problems, and talking with other fathers about their experiences broadened my views and understanding. Helped me to communicate better with my children.'

- 'The course has taught me to be a good listener and to pay more attention to what my children may be saying. It also helps me to be more tolerant and patient and it has helped in improving the 'behaviour' – both mine and the children's.'
- 'When I started the course I was hard-headed, but in the end the course has made me see things in a different light. Very good course.'
- 'The course has been quite helpful. Some of the things I learnt during the course were put into practice and it worked. And as they say the grass is greener on the other side. Given the time it will be greener.'
- 'I did not attend the course regularly because of my work, but still I feel I have learned from the course and understand my son more and help make him understand me.'

Trevor Collumbell, a social work student, did a research project on the outcomes for the group of Asian fathers quoted above. This project involved doing a 15-question in-depth interview with each parent to try to establish their views on the outcomes of their attendance on the course. The conclusion of the research was that the parents had found the group:

- Personally empowering
- Had improved their confidence and self-esteem
- Made them feel less isolated
- Made them more positive, calm and in control, resulting in a happier family life
- Made them more confident in their parenting role
- Improved relationships with their teenagers.

Our conclusion, from studying this research project and examining the evaluation form results, is that we need to do more work on redesigning our evaluation form. Whereas our current form places emphasis on the reduction of 'teenage behaviours', much of our work in groups with parents of teenagers suggests that, although the 'behaviours' themselves create conflict in families, it is the breakdown in communication and a rather more complex set of criteria that is upsetting to the parents. If the downward spiral of negative interactions that result in a very low quality of relationship between parents and teenagers can be reversed or slowed down, better feelings are created. Often the very behaviours which were originally so contentious are tolerated at the end of the day. Consequently, measuring reductions in 'behaviour' difficulties alone does not seem to be a good measure of the progress that parents have made while attending a group. For example, a parent may, during the course of a group, have learnt to communicate better with their teenager about the state of their bedroom, and had come to allow their teenager to have more responsibility for the tidiness (or lack of tidiness!) in their own room. This learning and practice may have dramatically improved the quality of the parent-teenager relationship, but may still lead the parent to view the less than tidy bedroom as a 'behaviour' difficulty. It follows that an evaluation form that only asks about 'behaviour' difficulties probably underestimates the complexity of the parent-teenager relationship, and underestimates the progress parents can make.

Identifying parents' needs and feelings

The list of negative parental thoughts and feelings listed below is extremely relevant to practitioners engaged in family work, as it identifies common parental needs which ought to be considered or addressed. Assessing experiences and stress factors which have generated negative thoughts and feelings is crucial, particularly in families where violence has become a pattern of behaviour. Such ways of thinking and feeling can be highly destructive to family relationships as they create a vicious circle, in which negative thoughts and feelings can become a self-fulfilling prophecy. In such situations everybody is the victim because the quality of family relationships becomes abusive to every person involved.

Statements in the list below were mainly gathered prior to the commencement of the groupwork programme, and are in stark contrast to the positive statements in the comments from Asian fathers above.

- Helplessness
- Powerlessness
- Loneliness
- 'What have I done to deserve this?'
- 'Nothing will ever change.'
- 'What do I do next?'
- 'I thought being a parent came naturally.'
- Frustration
- 'I hit out because I don't know what else to do!'
- 'My daughter knows the right buttons to push to get me wound up.'
- Inadequacy
- Isolation
- 'Why me?'
- 'He is like a devil.'
- 'It was never like this on TV.'
- 'My son hates me.'
- Resentment
- 'I feel like a coiled spring ready to explode.'
- 'Why are my friend's teenagers so nice?'
- 'I feel knackered and just a slave to my 12-year-old.'

Conclusion

The purpose of this chapter has been to promote a model of good practice and to demonstrate the usefulness of evaluation. It represents a set of principles and procedures which, if adhered to, facilitate planning, partnership and greater effectiveness. Such skills are vital when working within the principles of the Children Act.

Evaluation does not occur in a vacuum, as it represents a dynamic process clearly reflecting assessment and intervention. Future planning and the way a practitioner operates must also be informed by this process. We should not depend on our experience or professional instinct to tell us that our advice and intervention was right or effective, but we must instead generate clear evidence for our actions and results.

12 Parent support groups

The need for parent support groups

We have found that during the last six years of running fun and families groups, and more recently living with teenagers groups, the need for parent support groups have become more and more obvious, and we have listed below some of the reasons for this:

- Parents who have attended a living with teenagers group often feel quite bereft when the short seven-week course comes to an end. The support and friendship enjoyed becomes important to them. So, although a few parents need further advice and support from us, many benefit from just getting out regularly, keeping company with other people who have common interests, and taking some time for themselves away from the children.
- Some parents within the groups discover that certain of their difficulties arise from conflicting advice about teenage development. They therefore develop a need to keep in touch with 'informed' opinion and informal support which helps them select what is right for them and encourages, rather than criticises or questions their efforts.
- Many parents find that during the teenage years there are many issues that raise anxiety for parents and are sources of conflict for teenagers. These include school exams, bullying, drugs, sexuality, the influence of friends, clothing and handling money. Parents find themselves dealing with constantly shifting demands which make it very difficult to offer consistent responses. Parents find the opportunity to compare notes with other parents very reassuring.

- Many parents have friends who are too shy or reluctant to attend the group programme. Gradually, they have been prepared to come to a less formal support group and consequently derive benefit from doing so. Some parents have even joined a living with teenagers group as a result of this.
- Research undertaken by Andy Gill shows that parents who did have support of an informal group, maintained the progress they had achieved during the fun and family group far longer and more successfully than those who did not. Our experience of talking to parents who have continued to attend support groups for living with teenagers groups, suggests that similar advantages have applied to them.

How support groups have developed

At first, support groups for fun and families groups were explored by putting people in touch with another parent living in the same area. This became a type of 'buddy' system, but it had only limited success. We have found through experience, and trial and error, that support groups really take off when parents themselves take matters into their own hands and do not depend on the groupwork facilitators to set a group up. The original intention was to schedule the seventh session of the groupwork programme one month after the main agenda was finished. The idea here was to offer a chance to see how people were doing and to provide a booster or extra help if parents wanted this. The parents returned after the month and had obviously missed the group members and the weekly sessions. From this, parents began to think about forming their own support groups.

In rural Leicestershire, for example, meetings began in the parents' own homes. They began to invite speakers as well as using the meetings for purely social events. This meant that the topics and activities varied and were really what they wanted for themselves. In Bradford, a support group formed a lobby and got a petition together to the Housing Committee to improve the lot of those struggling in temporary housing accommodation. They were sure that little more could be done to help themselves and their children until their living conditions and housing needs were addressed. A Melton Mowbray group in Leicestershire arranged a programme of assertiveness training as a follow-on from a fun and families group. In the Wirral a 'Feeling good' programme was set up; this was to help parents to enjoy themselves and appreciate their own strengths and qualities. There has since been a follow-on course from this called 'Stay feeling good'.

Some practical points we have learned

Although the meetings held in individual homes flourished, it also became clear that some structure would be needed to help the group survive and gain the most advantage from their endeavours. Keeping in touch with each other and organising speakers all involved time and cost, such as telephone calls and postage. Therefore, small committees were formed and they acquired a certain amount of funding from local charities and Social Services community grants. Group leaders continued to offer encouragement, but parents designed and organised their own programmes. In one group, forty people were involved and meetings attracted between 8–20 participants.

Some parents began to publicise their group in the local free press and included a telephone number as a contact point. Funds were raised and stationary was printed. There also began to be a forum where new ideas and suggestions for improvement of the fun and families programme was generated. One example of this was the suggestion by parents that we should give certificates to parents who had completed the seven-week course.

The main practical issues that have consistently arisen revolve around:

- Finding a warm comfortable room to meet in
- Organising tea and coffee facilities
- Organising a crèche or childminding scheme
- Someone to be the secretary who will pull the group together and remind people what is happening each meeting
- Someone to act as treasurer if funding and fund raising is to be an issue
- Organising social activities if this is wanted
- Providing some programme or focus for meetings.

Some ideas for well-received topics

The range and extent of well-received topics has been wide. A group of Asian fathers of teenagers decided that they wanted to involve their whole family in the support group. They therefore decided to make the focus of the group regular social activities. They started by organising a tenpin bowling evening at the local Super Bowl. They also agreed that each parent should be able to bring a friend. In addition the two group leaders were invited to each meeting – which takes place roughly every two months – and allowed to bring a friend. This support group, which had its origins in January/ February 1996 is still meeting at the time of writing.

A group of white parents who were involved in a living with teenagers group between January and February 1997 decided to form a group to meet monthly. They were very happy with the idea of using the same room in a local community college that the group had been run in. The group leaders gave them the information about how to book the room and the names and addresses and address labels for all the group members. The group met monthly and every three months invited the three group leaders to join them for a session. The most significant aspect of this support group is that everybody has been consistent in their attendance, and the group members have recognised that the support of other parents is the most important aspect in helping them to feel confident about their role as parents.

Some lessons we have learned from parents

We have learned that trying to suggest or help setting up support groups ourselves does not work very well. The initiative needs to come from the parents themselves. The more effort the groupwork leaders put into setting them up, the more it seems that the parents feel the support group is almost a continuation of the living with teenagers course. They therefore come to rely on the leaders for ideas, suggestions, organisation and initiative. The parents feel more empowered and in control if the initiative comes from them. We have therefore strongly advocated this. A group in Hinckley found that by about the fifth session of the programme, parents began automatically to think about what would happen after the seven weeks were finished. From this, members began to think about a support group, so that by the end of the seven weeks they had already planned and organised their group. This was fully organised and run by themselves. They then went on to forming a women's group as a result of this process.

Generally support groups have been completely open. Anyone can join or leave as they choose. This has useful spin-offs, as some people then pluck up enough courage to join a living with teenagers group. A down side to such flexibility is that the burden of keeping the group going falls on a few willing shoulders, which inevitably means that such people move on to new interests and there have to be people willing to take over. However, this is generally the case with various types of groups whose life is limited and unpredictable. It has to be acknowledged that some groups of a support nature have a natural life of their own, and their winding-up may well be a sign that everybody involved has been able to obtain what they wanted from it. Group workers should not feel that if a group doesn't form, or doesn't keep meeting, that they are in any way responsible or should feel they have failed. It is very much like the old adage that 'you can take a horse to water but you can't make it drink'. In the end parents will only meet together if they want to, assuming that they have been supported in resolving all the practical issues referred to above.

The achievements of support groups

Parents involved in these groups gained considerable confidence. Some of them shared in presenting workshops at the inaugural conference of the Centre for Fun and Families. Others took part in and helped to produce a video on child behaviour. This video is now available for training and discussion work.

Parents from a very varied range of backgrounds have shared in the activities mentioned in this chapter. They have come from different social classes and ethnic groups. They have experienced varying degrees of difficulty with their children. Some very severe behaviour problems that have been made more acute by worrying medical conditions, have been addressed. Other parents have had mental health problems themselves. Some parents have come just because they want more information. There have also been those parents who felt defeated and in need of reassurance. Generally speaking, they have found it from others in the group.

The sharing and giving to each other has been an exhilarating and reciprocal experience. One parent observed, 'If a head teacher [who was in the group] can have problems, it cannot be so bad that I find it tough.' Another highly competent mum came to realise her own high expectations and standards were most unusual and were making a rod for her own back.

These lessons were learned without instruction. They happened because people were together and shared a sense of belonging. Meeting together has created loyalties and incentives. Many parents acknowledge they may have felt like giving up, but did not want to let their friends down or to lose face. Quite often, even those parents who already knew what to do to resolve their teenager's difficult behaviours became aware that 'going it alone' can erode resolve.

The rediscovery of energy has been amazing. People struggling with their own finances suddenly wanted to help raise money for the group, or other groups. Parents who felt they were now managing quite well, found time to visit someone else who just needed guidance and a little support and company. Generally, within the support groups, unexpected potential and enthusiasm has emerged and personal strength and growth has blossomed in a most moving way. After many years of running fun and families groups and living with teenagers groups, we now feel that support groups are a vital and natural complement to our groupwork programmes. We wholeheartedly welcome this development and feel that we have yet to see the full potential of the help parents can provide for others.

13 Future developments

In Chapter 1, Part 1, we listed the achievements the Centre had accomplished since its formation as a national voluntary organisation in June 1990. It is worth emphasising that it now has a range of contacts throughout the country, and produces regular newsletters to keep people aware of its developments and ourselves alert to the most promising project to pursue.

Future possibilities

The last seven years have demonstrated to the Centre that there is a consistently high demand for the training/consultancy and student placement services that the Centre provides. The demand from parents to attend group programmes continues to be very high, and the demands from the parents of children with disabilities shows every indication of being equally as high. The continued growth in demand in both areas indicates that the Centre is meeting needs that are *not* available to them from other statutory or voluntary agencies.

Within the Centre itself plans are not limited by a shortage of ideas about what we hope to achieve in the future. The main limitation is a shortage of money to take the ideas further and to make them a reality. From discussions we have had the staff see the following key developments as being on our agenda for the next two to three years.

National link person system

We feel that it is important to offer more support to workers from statutory and voluntary agencies who are running living with teenagers groups throughout the country. This system would allow good practice and new ideas about the programme to be shared nationwide.

Parent's manual

Initially centre group leaders were only able to provide parents with a folder to store papers, handouts or record charts during and after the group, so we developed a parent's manual for the fun and families programme using a 'ring-binder' type of cover. This allowed papers and charts to be kept safely and in logical order and sequence. It also gave the material a more professional appearance. However, we want to avoid a glossy printed manual. This is mainly because the moment it is printed it would become out of date and inflexible. In addition, the glossy manual gives the impression of being a 'teaching aid' or 'expert's manual', which is a concept the group programme is attempting to avoid. We would like to extend this concept to include a parent's manual for the living with teenagers programme.

Anti-discriminatory practice

Within our Action Plan we intend to expand in the following areas. First, we would wish to achieve the translation of a much greater percentage of our material into other languages. Second, we would like to run groups for parents of African-Caribbean origin to test its applicability within these communities. Third, we would like to further develop the fun and families and living with teenagers programmes to make them more relevant to parents of children with disabilities. Finally, we would like to make links with organisations that represent gay people, to attempt to discover their preferences in terms of the groupwork services the Centre can offer to gay parents.

Parental involvement

The Centre has attempted to involve parents who have attended groups in a variety of ways. First, we have promoted the running of their own parent support groups after the groupwork programme finishes. Second, we have asked parents to attend the first session of new groups to motivate new parents and to tell the participants how they benefited from the group. Third, we have attempted to persuade parents to join the Centre's

Governing Body and to become involved in the Centre's fund-raising activities. Finally, parents are encouraged to use their talents and skills to promote the work of the Centre. For example, one parent who was a yoga teacher ran a part-session on relaxation. Another parent with artistic skills designed and produced the Centre's Fun Stickers and Albums. However, we feel that some parents could play a part in running a living with teenagers group, and also subsequently assist us in our training activities. We feel this is an aim we would like to achieve, despite the fact that there are many practical obstacles.

Permanent funding

Until recently the Centre received no regular funding from any statutory body. This year we have managed to obtain two-year funding from one charitable trust, and also a three-year recurrent grant from the Department of Health. While receiving funding is not an end in itself, but a means to achieving the objectives set out above, it is an important aim for the Centre to acquire some reasonably secure, stable and regular form of funding. This would be useful because it would encourage the Centre to plan in a more systematic and long-term way. Unstable funding tends to produce more of a crisis management approach, which does not lead to the best use of the Centre's staff resources. Consequently, the aims set out above are much more likely to be achieved if a substantial and stable source of funding is found.

Concluding remarks

In this chapter on future developments we have, hopefully, given you an insight into aspects of our work that are likely to be developed over the next few years. In addition, we hope we have raised your enthusiasm for running living with teenagers groups for parents. Furthermore, we hope we have raised your enthusiasm to the point that you want to do more than read about it and to start thinking about when you are going to run your first group. Or, if you have already run one, to start planning your next one.

The other most important message we hope to have conveyed is that you are not alone. If you run into difficulties, or would like to talk to someone else who has run a group, you are welcome to contact the Centre and we will either try to answer your query or put you in touch with someone locally in your region who you can talk to. There is also a list of resources available from the Centre to assist you in your work in Appendix D.

We would like to conclude by offering the observation that, in the last decade, crisis interventions into the lives of families with teenagers have been over-dominant as a form of professional intervention. Sadly, this style of work has proved both unsuccessful, highly unpopular with families and very negative for the professional staff who have to undertake such work. Recently reported studies show that 'Many of the cases involving teenagers in crisis were known to social services, but professional support was rare and previous requests for assistance from parents frequently failed to result in any practical help (Sinclair *et al.*, 1995). As a result, when social workers did intervene and offer services, many parents were exhausted and disillusioned, and saw accommodation as the only remaining option' (Department of Health, 1996).

In offering a model of work that shows family support can be economical, efficient and effective and also fun, we hope we have made some contribution to turning the tide towards a more positive approach that is in keeping with the expressed wishes of parents of teenagers.

Appendices

Appendix A: Teenage behaviour and communication rating scale

On the next page are a series of phrases that describe teenage behaviour. Please circle the number describing how often behaviours currently affecting you occur. Also, circle 'yes' or 'no' to indicate whether or not the behaviour is currently a problem for you.

How often does this occur with your teenager?

	Never	Seldom	Sometimes	Often	Always	Is this a problem?	
	1	**2**	**3**	**4**	**5**	**Yes**	**No**
1 Refuses to do chores when asked							
2 Refuses to go to bed on time							
3 Stays out late							
4 Does not obey house rules							
5 Refuses to obey until threatened with punishment							
6 Acts defiantly when asked to do something							
7 Argues with parents about rules							
8 Gets angry when doesn't get own way							
9 Cheeky to adults							
10 Uses bad language							
11 Hits parents							
12 Steals							
13 Lies							
14 Refuses to tidy up							
15 Ignores requests							
16 Continually interrupts conversations							
17 Verbally fights with sister or brother							
18 Physically fights with sister or brother							
19 Doesn't appear to listen							

Other behaviour problems. . . . .
. . . .

Below are a series of questions relating to communication. Please indicate the number which best represents your current situation, and also whether or not you believe it is a problem.

	Never	Seldom	Sometimes	Often	Always	Is this a problem?	
	1	2	3	4	5	Yes	No
1 Are you able to listen to younger people's point of view?							
2 Do you praise and encourage your offspring?							
3 Do you reward good behaviour?							
4 Are you able to negotiate with them?							
5 Can you reach a compromise or agreement?							
6 Can you express yourself without losing your temper?							

Thank you

Date ......

Appendix B: Sample press release

Bringing up Teenagers Can Be Fun

Being a parent is the hardest job in the world and everybody is willing to criticise you, including your own teenagers. Bringing up teenagers requires amazing patience, tact and the ability to love the unwashed, untidy, uncommunicative and at times the unlovable! However, if you feel you are out of your depth or it is all too much, help is at hand. The Centre for Fun and Families, a national voluntary organisation, is running a course for parents and teenagers. The course is being run at Guthlaxton Community College in Wigston on Wednesday evening between 7pm – 9pm. It starts on January 8 and runs for 7 weeks. The course is free and hopes to cater for between 8–10 parents.

From six years of experience of running courses for parents, the Centre staff have found that the sorts of behaviours that parents of teenagers are often trying to cope with include violence, swearing, defiance, school refusal, sulking or eating difficulties. However, parents who attend the courses are pleased to find that behaviour difficulties can be reduced by an average of 50% by attending the seven-week course.

In addition most parents feel much less anxious because they are able to discover they are not the only ones dealing with these problems. They also find that they are the real experts on their own teenagers, and that sharing the task of parenting together in a group enables them to discover which of their own solutions work best. Parents meeting together generate tremendous enthusiasm and support, which help them achieve very satisfying results. An additional bonus is that those who attend the course even enjoy it! If you would like to make a positive start to the New Year, and make the best of your relationships with your teenagers, please come along.

If you are interested in attending the course, or would like more information, please ring David Neville, Centre for Fun and Families, on Leicester 270 7198.

Appendix C: Sample certificate

has been awarded a

Fun and Families

Certificate

for completing the seven-week course

"Living with Teenagers"

Date...... Signed...........

25 Shanklin Drive, Leicester LE2 3RH   0116 270 7198

Appendix D: Summary of resources

Promoting Positive Parenting   £14.95

Written by the Centre staff, Dick Beak, Liz King and David Neville, this book was published by Arena Publications in 1995. It is designed as a guide for professional staff who want to run fun and families groups. Part I of the book gives information about the background of the Centre for Fun and Families. Part II covers the theoretical background, including issues related to empowerment, anti-discriminatory practice, social learning theory, the role of cognitive behavioural theory, groupwork skills and giving structure to groups for parents. Part III gives a complete guide to each of the sessions of the seven-week programme. Part IV discusses issues related to evaluation and the setting up of parent support groups. The final part offers further information about the Centre's resources and plans for future developments within the Centre.

Booklets   £3.00 each

The Centre has produced the following comprehensive range of booklets to cover most of the skill and practice areas that are relevant to staff running groupwork programmes:

Planning a fun and families group

This offers a planning checklist for staff who want to set up a group. It deals with practical matters, including the race, gender and disability issues that need to be addressed.

Living with teenagers: a bridge over troubled waters

A practical guide to help parents and young people sort out their disagreements.

Working together

Reprinted with new drawings to reflect a multi-cultural society, this step-by-step guide for parents and professionals on strategies aims to help parents increase desirable behaviour and decrease unwanted behaviour. Available in Gujarati and Urdu.

Basics of social learning theory

A straightforward, 'jargon-free', description of the theoretical model used in the groupwork programme run by the Centre.

Parent support groups

A description of the self-help support groups that have developed for parents who have taken part in the Centre's groupwork programme.

Evaluation: measuring effectiveness in work with children and families

Offers a range of methods for evaluating both group and individual work with families.

An introduction to cognitive behavioural work

More advanced theory to assist group leaders see how parent's thoughts and feelings can affect how they respond to their children or young people.

Groupwork skills: giving structure to groups

A review of the skills required to run fun and families groups. Deals with the tasks and roles of group leaders, effective group interventions and dealing with problems.

Anti-discriminatory practice

Offers ideas on how to ensure that groupwork services can be offered to all members of a local community. It also includes a case study on the practical application of these ideas to the Centre's development of services to the Asian community.

Working with parents with children with disabilities

This new booklet is intended to be used in conjunction with the guidance offered in *Promoting Positive Parenting* and provides ideas about adapting the groupwork programme to meet the specific needs of parents with children with disabilities.

Games and exercises used in a fun and families group

Gives details of all the games and exercises, including the learning objectives.

Video and audio material

The Centre makes considerable use of video recording as a way of helping parents develop their parenting skills. Video and audio material is also used as a means of making the groupwork programme more interesting for parents.

A video helps to demonstrate a range of methods of coping with child behaviour difficulties. Using a video is also an invaluable means of generating discussion among parents within the group setting. The Centre currently produces:

'The 5 Excerpts' video   £12.00

A 30-minute tape, which gives a selection of the video material used in the running of both the fun and families and living with teenagers programmes. It provides a number of scenarios on one tape, avoiding the need to purchase and carry around several different videos, all needing to be set to the right point to play!

Relaxation tape   £7.50

An audio tape designed to help parents relax. It has been found to be helpful to both parents and group leaders!

These video and audio resources are particularly valuable because:

- Both video and audio tapes can be used when working with families on both an individual and groupwork basis.
- They have been designed to be used in conjunction with the Centre's programmes.
- All of these products represent excellent value for money.

Training packs for group leaders   £9.50

Packs are available to assist staff involved in setting up and running both 'Fun and Families' and 'Living with Teenagers' groups. They provide invaluable material, such as handouts for parents and guidance for group leaders on some of the practical issues involved in running a group. They provide a week by week guide to each session of the group specifically for leaders. The packs also give information about ways of evaluating the effectiveness of the group. The Fun and Families Pack is available in Gujarati.

Fun Stickers and Album   £2.50

The fun stickers provide a positive way of helping parents to get the fun back into caring for their children. The stickers and album have been designed especially for the Centre for Fun and Families for use by parents undertaking the groupwork programmes. Each pack contains two sets of fun stickers, two albums and guidance for parents on their use.

Parent's guide   £10.50

This guide is produced in a ring binder. It is intended for use by parents involved in the 'Fun and Families' groupwork programme and takes parents through the ideas presented in this particular course. It provides a safe place for handouts given each week, and includes a Fun Stickers and Album Pack and a copy of the booklet 'Working Together'.

Consultancy service

The Centre offers a consultancy service for staff in different agencies, who may be involved in setting up and running a group. The aim of this service is to give individualised help to agencies to assist staff in effectively planning a successful start to their project and to offer advice and guidance if any difficulties arise during the course of the groupwork programme. Centre staff are able either to come to your agency or can arrange for your staff to visit the Centre. If you are interested, please contact the Centre for more details.

References and further reading

Adams, R. (1990) *Self Help, Social Work and Empowerment*. Birmingham: BASW.

Ahmad, B. (1990) *Black Perspectives in Social Work*. Birmingham: Ventura Press.

Anderson J., Osada and Thompson, N. (1994) 'Teaching Anti-Discriminatory Practice', *Practice Teaching in Social Work*. Birmingham: Pepar.

Beck, A.T. (1976) *Cognitive Therapy and the Emotional Disorders*. New York: New American Library.

Beresford, P. and Croft, S. (1990) *From Paternalism to Participation*. London: Open Services Project.

Davis, L. and Proctor, E. (1989) *Race, Gender and Class; Guidelines for practice with Individuals, Families and Groups*. London: Prentice-Hall.

Department of Health (1996) *Focus on Teenagers, Research into Practice*. Norwich: HMSO.

Douglas, T. (1991) *A Handbook of Common Groupwork Problems*. London: Routledge.

Dominelli, L. (1988) *Anti-Racist Social Work*. London: Macmillan.

Dryden, W. and Scot, M. (1990) *An Introduction to Cognitive-Behaviour Therapy: Theory and Applications*. Liverpool: Liverpool Personal Services Society and Gale Centre Publications.

Eyeberg, S. *et al.* (1980) 'Inventory of Child Problem Behaviours', *Journal of Clinical Child Psychology*, Spring, pp. 22–9.

Evan, G. and Grant, L. (1995) *Moyenda Project Report 1991–1994*. Exploring Parenthood, London.

Falloon, I. *et al.* (1984) *Family Care of Schizophrenia*. New York: Guilford Press.

Foster, S.L. (1985) *Workshop Outline Assessing and treating Parent-Adolescent Conflict*. West Virginia University: Department of Psychology.

Gambrill, E.D. (1977) *Behaviour Modification Handbook of Assessment, Intervention and Evaluation*. San Francisco and London: Jossey Bass.

Gill, A. (1989) *Groupwork Programme Evaluation Questionnaire*. Leicester: Centre for Fun and Families.

Gill, A. (1989a) 'Putting fun back into families', *Social Work Today*, 4 May.

Gill, A. (1989) *Questionnaire to Measure Parental Attitudes, Attributions and Emotional Feelings*. Leicester: Centre for Fun and Families.

Gill, A. (1989) *Structured Observation of Parent-Child Interaction*. Leicester: Centre for Fun And Families.

Hawton, Kirk, Clarke (1990) *Cognitive Behaviour Therapy for Psychiatric Problems: A Practical Guide*. Oxford: Oxford University Press.

Herbert, M. (1978) *Conduct Disorders of Childhood and Adolescence: A Behavioural Approach to Assessment and Treatment*. Chichester: Wiley.

Herbert. M. (1988) *Working with Children and their Families*. London: Routledge.

Herbert, M. (1991) *Child Care and the Family*. A Client Management Resource Pack. Windsor: Nfer-Nelson.

MacDonald, S. (1991) *All Equal under the Act?* London: Race Equality Unit, National Institute for Social Work.

Martin, P. and Bateson, P. (1986) *Measuring Behaviour*. Cambridge: Cambridge University Press.

Meichenbaum, D. (1985) *Stress Inoculation Training*. New York: Pergamon (Currently Available 1995 Alklyn and Bacon £14.95)

Naag, R. (1997) *To Examine the Effectiveness of Parent Training*. Unpublished Dissertation, Department of Behavioural Studies, Nene College.

Neville, D., King, L. and Beak, D. (1995) *Promoting Positive Parenting*. Aldershot: Arena, Ashgate Publishing Limited.

Novaco, R.W. (1985) *Anger, Stress and Coping with Provocation: An Instructional Manual*. Unpublished Manual, University of California: Irvine.

Paterson, G. R. (1974) 'Retraining of Aggressive Boys by their Parents: Review of recent literature and follow up evaluation', *Journal of the Canadian Psychiatric Association*, Vol. 19, No. 2, pp. 142–57.

Preston-Shoot, M. (1987) *Effective Groupwork*. London: BASW Publications, Macmillan Education Ltd.

Rogers, C. R. (1977) *Client Centred Therapy*. London: Constable.

Sacks, O. (1991) *Seeing Voices*. London: Picador.

Scott, M. J. *et al.* (1995) *Developing Cognitive-Behavioural Counselling*. London and New Delhi: Sage Publications.

Scott, M. (1989) *A Cognitive Approach to Clients Problems*. London and New York: Tavistock Routledge.

Sheldon, B. (1982) *Behaviour Modification: Theory, Practice and Philosophy*. London: Tavistock.

Solomon, B. (1976) *Black Empowerment: Social Work in oppressed communities*. New York: Columbia University Press.

Thompson, N. (1993) *Anti-Discriminatory Practice*. London: Macmillan.